Time Management and Stop Procrastination 2-in-1 Book

Discover The Most Effective Time Management Strategies and Learn How to Avoid the Number 1 Productivity Killer: Procrastination

Time Management

Discover The Secrets to Beat The Clock Learn How to Be in Control of Your Time, Maximize Your Day, Boost Productivity and Still Have Time to Enjoy Your Friends & Family

Table of Contents

Introduction 7
Chapter 1 – Stop Wasting Time 11
    The Importance of Time Management 11
    Signs You're Failing at Managing Your Time 13
    The Reasons Why You're Failing 19
    7 Big Myths About Time Management 21
Chapter 2 - Getting Things Done 101 23
    Essential Tips for Getting Things Done 23
    Essential Rules for Successful Time Management 25
    5 Lesser-Known Productivity Hacks You Need to Know 31
Chapter 3 - A Guide to Goal-Setting 39
    All About the Goal-Setting Theory of Motivation 39
    Goal-Setting Principles 40
    15 of the Best Tips for Effective Goal-Setting 47
    8 Common Reasons Why To-Do Lists Fail 50
Chapter 4 - The Secrets of Productivity 55
    How to Prioritize When Everything Is Important 55
    The Chunking Technique for Making Your Goals Achievable 63
    5 of the Biggest Productivity Killers and How to Overcome Them
.... 68
Chapter 5 - Dealing with Distractions 71
    The Difference Between Internal and External Distractions 71
    Types of Internal Distractions 73

13 Ways to Silence Internal Distractions 77
6 Reliable Ways to Defeat External Distractions 82

Chapter 6 - Emulating Success 86
Goal Setting Examples from The Business Masters 86
13 Time Management Hacks of Successful People 89
10 Morning Routines of Groundbreaking Entrepreneurs 93

Chapter 7 - Regaining Control of The Future 97
15 Effective Time Management Habits 97
Defeating Perfectionism Once and for All 101
Tools and Techniques to Take Back Time for Good 106

Conclusion 113

Introduction

The only resource you can't barter, buy or borrow is time. It doesn't even follow one of the fundamental laws of supply and demand: high demand causes supply to increase and meet the demand. While we all have access to the same amount of time each day —1,440 minutes — we use our time differently.

Your success or failure in life depends mainly on your time management capabilities. To be successful, you need to invest significant amounts of time to achieve your goal or improve your weaknesses. At certain seasons, I spent more time than my competitors so that I can have the edge over them in the marketplace. I didn't assume that I was mentally superior to my competitors; I only spent time more effectively to balance the playing field.

You need to spend balance the time you spend at home and the time you spend at work. If not, you will be successful in one and be a failure in the other. Fear not; this book will show you how to balance your work and home effectively. I congratulate you on investing in your life and success by reading this book.

If you are reading this, it's probably because:

- You want to be confident that you can take proper care of yourself and your family
- You desire long-lasting success in your career and personal life
- You want your friends and families to be proud of you and your accomplishments

Here's what you're probably doing right in your life:

Time Management

Since you are serious about improving your life experience, you are possibly implementing these basic career success strategies:

- You ensure that your performance at work exceeds the expectations of your bosses
- You arrive early and when needed, work overtime
- You are continually improving yourself to improve your work performance
- You seek mentors and network with your peers

The truth is, none of these actions will lift you to the personal or professional lifestyle you desire and deserve. Why? Let me explain:

For all things to function correctly, there has to be a balance. Let's use the washing machine's spin cycle as an illustration. When there are too many towels on one side of the tub, it slams, bangs and vibrates. If you don't fix it in time, the bearings will break, and the repairs can be expensive.

Your life can be likened to the washing machine. If you only focus and implement the necessary success steps of most people, you will achieve the same level of success as them. Thus, you may never accomplish everything you want or need in life. Your life will be completely imbalanced.

Over time, you will start getting drained spiritually, physically and emotionally. Consequently, you may begin to experience social problems, relationship problems, and health problems such as depression, diabetes, heart diseases, and high blood pressure. When you continuously live a life out of balance, you may never achieve your set goals or ambitions.

For centuries, the Chinese have known and have been implementing the yin and yang principle. The principle states that "two halves that complement each other produces wholeness." The keyword here is "wholeness." The two halves are your mind and your body; they work together to make your life whole.

If your life is not whole, you are not different from the wet towels swinging around the washing machine.

Let me tell you a secret: every successful person you have met and will ever meet are masters of productivity. If an expert should hand you the complete guide to success through proper time management, would you implement the steps in the guide?

- Will you use the secrets to increase your productivity and raise your success level?
- If you discover the productivity secrets of the most successful people, will you implement these secrets?
- I am willing to show you exactly what I do daily to consistently achieve my career and personal goals to live the kind of lifestyle you seek. Are you willing to follow these steps faithfully?

If your answer is yes to these three questions, then, you are ready to reach a new level of success with *Time Management: Proven Steps and Strategies for Managing Your Time Efficiently and Effectively*. This book

- Isn't just some rah-rah cheerleader guide that excites you with biographies and quotes of successful people. You won't find the typical "secrets to time management" that are copied and pasted articles from the internet and thrown together like some cheap pulp fiction novel.
- Details my exact daily actions and by all means, I am a successful and fulfilled person
- Shows you how to prioritize when everything is important

- Delves into the techniques for making your goals achievable
- Takes you deep into the biggest productivity killers and how to overcome them
- Helps you with ways to silence internal distractions
- Tells you reliable ways to defeat external distractions
- Contains goal-setting examples from the business masters
- Discusses time management hacks of successful people
- Takes you deep into the morning routines of groundbreaking entrepreneurs

I won't call this book a life-changing book. I will instead call it a life-enhancing book. With it, you start with the life you've built and elevated it to the levels you desire by implementing the exact steps of truly successful people.

In this book, you will find the precise information you need. You can start from the first page or read on topics that cause you the most challenge. I can assure you that this book will help you to maximize the scant 24 hours we all have per day.

For instance, you can check out chapter one for signs that suggest your time management sucks! Also, in chapter three, you will discover common reasons why you can't do anything with your to-do lists.

The point is, regardless of the chapter you choose to start reading, you will discover lots of valuable steps you can implement. Thus, you can increase your performance without increasing your work hours.

Chapter 1 – Stop Wasting Time

The Importance of Time Management

By definition, time management is a process of organizing and planning your time between specific activities to achieve efficiency.

Time is valuable to us whether or not we assign a dollar value to it. Think about the number of times you complained about having insufficient time to reach a goal or complete a task during this past week. If you don't fully understand why it's crucial for you to manage your time better, then, taking measures such as downloading time management apps, creating lists or adjusting your sleep time won't help you to solve your problems. First, take a look at the big picture to understand what you will gain from managing your time effectively. Here are eight critical reasons why you need to manage your time effectively:

1. **Prevent procrastination**

You leave no room for procrastination when you practice proper time management. You will become more self-disciplined as you become better at managing your time. Thus, you can become self-disciplined in other areas of your life where you lack discipline.

2. **Find the time to relax**

Due to family responsibilities, errands and jobs, the majority of us don't get sufficient time to relax and unwind. We struggle to find just 10 minutes to sit down and do nothing. With proper time management practices, you will get more done during the day and create the time to relax, unwind and prepare for a good night's sleep later in the day.

3. Avoid stress

It's easy to feel rushed and overwhelmed when you are not in control of your time. Thus, you will start struggling to complete your tasks. Imagine you were making frantic efforts to finish a project to avoid missing a close deadline. Then, your boss drops a new job on your desk and asks you how soon you can complete the new task. What will be your response?

However, when you can manage your time, you will complete most projects before their deadlines. You can adequately estimate the period you will use to complete a task and be confident in meeting deadlines.

4. Take advantage of learning opportunities

You become more valuable to your employer as you improve your repertoire. But if you don't have the time to enhance your knowledge, how can you become more relevant to your employer? Once you practice excellent time management skills, you can take advantage of great learning opportunities around you.

It doesn't mean going back to obtain additional certificates. Learning can be as simple as volunteering to host your company's open house. It can also be having lunch with colleagues in other departments to gain further insights into what they do. When you have adequate knowledge about your company and your industry, you have a higher chance of moving up the corporate ladder quickly.

5. Be in control of your life

Rather than following others blindly, time management allows you to control your life the way you want it. Thus, you make more sound decisions and accomplish more every day. Hence, the leaders in your industry will start seeking your help to get things done. With this increased exposure, you become perfectly placed for advanced opportunities.

6. Improve your decision-making

Regardless of the time management techniques you adopt, one significant side benefit of good time management practice is that you start making better decisions. When you don't have the time to consider your options before making a decision, you jump into conclusions and make poor decisions. Through effective time management, you feel more in control and can thoroughly examine your options before making a decision.

7. Improve your focus

When you are in control of your time, your concentration improves, and your efficiency is enhanced. Thus, you can complete your daily tasks quickly and effectively.

Do you want to consistently complete more tasks than anybody else? Do you seek promotion or awards? Then, you need to find the means to manage your time.

Signs You're Failing at Managing Your Time

Do you:

- Constantly have more to do than the time to them?
- Not rest from the time you wake up to the time you sleep in the night?
- Always feel tired after each day's work?

One vital attribute of a skilled manager is effectiveness. If you intend to accomplish a goal and you are not completing the right tasks to accomplish that goal, you won't accomplish it.

Here are some of the most common signs that you're failing at managing your time:

Time Management

1. No task delegation

You need to identify tasks that you can delegate, automate or outsource and remove them from your workload. Here are examples of tasks that you can delegate:

- Your most time-consuming tasks. These tasks could be customer research, developing a marketing strategy, collation and presentation of data, traffic generation and improvement of click-through rate.
- Tasks others might enjoy. You may have become bored with a task after completing it repeatedly. Hence, if you think some of your colleagues could enjoy it, delegate such task to them. Also, if a colleague should volunteer for a task, allow him to perform it.
- Tasks in which teammates have better skills. Devote your time to other things and allow teammates with better skills to handle tasks that suit their skills and abilities. Avoid being the competition for your teammates. If they are better at a task than you, let them have it.
- Fun tasks. Your teammates are likely to take offense when you perform all the enjoyable tasks and ask them to deal with the tedious tasks. Why keep the fun to yourself? Let them share in the fun.
- Regular tasks. These are recurring tasks (weekly or monthly) and things that must be done after completing a project.

2. Agreeing to everyone

If you continuously agree to do things for everyone, excluding your loved ones, you won't have the time to improve your life or have the time for your loved ones. If you're always helping others without working on the important tasks assigned to you, you will constantly have an excessive workload. Being assertive and learning to say "no" is one of the best ways to improve your time management.

While it is great to help your teammates at work, it should only be an occasional occurrence. If it becomes a regular occurrence, you're doing their job for them and no longer helping them. They need to figure out how to work without continually requesting for your help. Otherwise, they also have time management problems, and they need to deal with it fast.

3. Indecision

Have you experienced spending lots of time to consider various options but still can't make a decision? It is a sign that you have poor time management. This sign is related to having ill-defined goals. When your goals are clearly defined, you have a basis for choosing your next most important task at any given time. The next task is often chosen based on the ROI. For example, assuming you are to choose between two 1-hour tasks. Task A will give you an ROI of $100, while task B will provide you with an ROI of $150. If your goal is to make more money, your obvious choice is task B.

Tasks vary in time of execution and costs. Also, you may have restrictions on the next task to be performed due to resources available, energy levels and other factors. After a clearly-defined goal, here's one question you can ask to make an easy decision on the next task to perform. "Using the time and resources currently available to me, what's the most important task I can complete?"

4. Perfectionism

When tasks take too long to achieve or even fail because you wanted to ensure that everything is perfect, you are a poor time manager. When you are overwhelmed by the need for perfection, you fail to realize that very few tasks are performed flawlessly in reality. By making unrealistic demands from your teammates, your desire for perfection can destroy your relationships with them. If you berate your colleagues when they fail to reach your perfect standards, you will struggle to find colleagues willing to work with you.

Since you can't maintain cordial working relationships with your colleagues, you will always have time management problems. You can't do everything by yourself. You should realize that perfection is impossible and, most times, unnecessary. Only demand the best from your colleagues for each task. Then, using the feedback from completed tasks, you can make the necessary improvements.

Bear in mind that a perfect job that never gets completed is useless compared to an average job that meets the deadline.

5. Productivity decline

When you manage your time poorly, you miss deadlines; you have an increase in backlog and your productivity declines. Time management and energy management are equally important. If you can't do anything with your energy levels, merely organizing your time is a waste of effort. Once you have reduced energy levels, you start having poor time management. Hence, you are under intense pressure to complete tasks without missing the required deadline. This even sucks up more of your energy levels.

Track your energy levels when you struggle to find the cause of your poor time management. Seek ways to improve your energy management.

6. Ill-defined goals

You can only prioritize when you have clearly defined goals. Consequently, you can complete your tasks on time. Each goal should have a clearly defined outline - what to achieve, when to achieve it and the order of importance. You need to set clearly-defined goals around your schedule of activities. Thus, you gain clarity on what needs to be done and when you need to do it.

According to the 80/20 principle, not all tasks carry equal importance. On average, 20% of your efforts will be responsible for 80% of your results. The smallest percentage of the tasks you perform will be responsible for the most significant percentage of the results you will achieve. You can only identify the 80/20 tasks when you have clearly-defined goals. A side benefit is that you will eliminate time-consuming tasks.

7. Finding excuses

The pressure of failing to meet a deadline makes you impatient. Hence, you start finding reasons for failing to complete your deadlines. Most people attribute their poor time management to people, technology or both. But the truth is, if you have failed to manage your time correctly, people and technology cannot help you. Ensure that you are only working on essential tasks that you can complete using the time and resources available to you.

You will ruin your ability to focus on the crucial task by adding an unneeded deadline. Assuming there is a task that needs to be completed by the close of business tomorrow, but you decided to shift the deadline to close of business today without being pressured to do so. You would only be putting yourself under unnecessary pressure and rushing to complete the task. While on the contrary, it would have been best for you to spread the task's process between today and tomorrow.

8. Hastiness

When you rush tasks, it is a sign that you don't have enough time for these tasks or meet the expectations of these tasks. While some tasks require some rush, you shouldn't be rushing to complete all your assigned tasks. You should have ample time between tasks to deal with unanticipated circumstances.

For example, a previous meeting exceeded its allotted time. If you leave every task to the last minute, you will continuously be in a rush. What you fail to realize is that if meeting A runs late, meeting B will start late, and you have to spend your rest period to complete your assigned task for the day.

9. Tardiness

When you can't allot sufficient time to appointments or tasks, you are unable to complete these tasks or fail to meet appointments. Your peers assume you are irresponsible. In some cases, your tardiness may be a motivation problem. You can't motivate yourself to get out of bed and do what you're supposed to do. One primary reason for your motivation problem may be a misalignment between your goals and your time management objectives.

Your best option is to prioritize your goals and manage your time to achieve these goals. When you schedule a goal that isn't your priority, you lose the motivation to be punctual since you fail to realize the importance of the task. Hence, you come up short at tasks without feeling any remorse, and you're known for your frequent poor time management practice.

The truth is, when you are punctual, it shows you respect your colleagues. The reverse is also true: when you are late, it is a sign that you disrespect your colleagues. Rather than being late for tasks that seem unimportant to you, you can decline to undertake the task.

The Reasons Why You're Failing

There are times we struggle to control our daily affairs despite our best efforts to efficiently organize our time, stay ahead of schedule or complete tasks successfully. Rather than creating additional to-do lists, you must identify the source of time management issues. Where is your time slipping away, and what are you doing wrong?

Let's take a look at eight reasons why you're failing at time management:

1. No plan at all
You need a proper method to change something already in motion in your life. Don't expect everything to fix itself. Create a timetable that makes you accountable for every hour of your day. Don't deviate from your daily plan, refer to it and review it. Thus, you can start developing and incorporating new habits into your day.

2. Procrastination
Start implementing your scheme immediately. Don't wait for the new month, Sunday or the next milestone in your life before making a change. The main idea is for you to act on the plan.

3. No grace
Since you're not perfect, there are times you will mess up. However, it doesn't mean you're a failure, or your hard work isn't paying off. So, give yourself the grace to get up the next day and be better.

4. Lack of accountability
Ask a trusted colleague to make you accountable for your daily actions. If you are late, mention it to the trusted colleague. Then, make a plan for what happens when you fail to meet your set expectations.

5. No motivation

The comments from your coworkers shouldn't motivate you. Decide on your motivation and ensure it's the right kind of motivation. Examples of strong motivators are personal development, excellence and well-being. Changes you make for your well-being will become a lifestyle change, but changes made for someone else won't last.

6. Making unnecessary changes

Concentrate on one specific goal at a time. If your objective is to get to work on time, identify the cause of your lateness to work. Then, eliminate it. Make it a priority to determine the necessary changes you need to make. Making unnecessary changes won't lead to new habits. For instance, spending two hours on Facebook early in the morning can cause you to be late for work. You can switch that up and spend two hours on Facebook the previous night. If the changes are necessary, make them a priority.

7. Unrealistic expectations

Don't over-expect. If you usually wake up at 7:45 am and get to work by 8.15 instead of 8 am, then, you can't suddenly start waking up at 5 am. It won't work that way. Your best option is to start learning how to wake up at 7 am. Then, slowly work your way up till you start waking up at 5:30 am.

8. Implementing a lot at once

One big mistake when addressing an issue in your life is to make a long list of things to change. Then, trying to take action on all these things at once on the next day. That's an entirely wrong approach. Your first step is to learn how to get out of bed on time. Then, seek to achieve the next goal. Over time, you would have developed new habits.

7 Big Myths About Time Management

In today's always-on business world, time management is crucial than ever. Though most professionals offer various tips to prioritize and balance work tasks and the home front, most of these tips are myths and poor advice that could have a negative impact than a positive one.

Here are the top seven myths you shouldn't buy about time management:

1. "Budget your time."
Don't be surprised when your budget gets shot 15 minutes into the day. Instead, create regular chunks of time in which you will make sufficient progress before moving to the next goal. During these chunks of periods, don't take calls, answer emails or check your social media page. Doing this helps you to avoid random interruptions rather than 'got a minute' meetings.

2. "Plan your day."
This was the mantra of time management. However, you may never get close to your long-term goals by using daily plans. Why? You finish each day with additional to-dos which you add to the next day's list until you give up on your long-term goals. A simple and effective solution is to include your long-term goals into your weekly plans.

3. "A detailed task list is essential to manage your time."
It is more important to structure your tasks in line with your strategic objectives rather than just listing them. You can become a master of time management by using 15 minutes before your bedtime the previous day to plan your next day to meet a defined expectation. You increase your decision-making and productivity by limiting your planning time.

4. "A structured day means a well-managed time."

For optimum results, time management, efficiency, effectiveness and productivity depend on each individual. There is no one-size-fits-all proposition. You need to find out what works for you.

5. "There's always time for your priorities."

You can still feel stressed despite knowing your priorities and aligning your activities with them. Bear in mind that you can only change how you feel about the time you have, but you can't change the time. It will always feel stressful to think you have insufficient time. Instead, tell yourself, "I have all the time I need to accomplish my desires." by doing this, you are more present and open to new, different solutions, you become more present and feel calmer. Thus, you can get more done.

6. "Schedule your hardest tasks first."

A recipe for procrastination is to attempt a tough task when you are rock bottom energy levels. If your energy is typically high at midnight, focus on the most challenging projects during this time. If you're usually flat on Thursday afternoon, schedule less important meetings for that day.

7. "Better time management is a result of better task management."

Though I am a fan of time blocking for managing priorities, I still believe that we need to make intentional choices on where to focus our energy before we can have proper time management. Since our choices define our priorities, we need to make better choices to have better time management.

Chapter 2 - Getting Things Done 101

Essential Tips for Getting Things Done

Getting things done, or GTD, is a reasonably simple method contrary to what you may think. It involves using simple rules to manage a few lists. Anyone, regardless of their background, can understand and apply these rules.

However, you need to develop at least one of the three habits for getting things done. Hence, the complicated part of GTD is in practice and not getting things done. Here those three habits:

1. **Keep your head empty**

"An empty mind is open to everything and ready for anything." - Shunryu Suzuki

David Allen is the author of *Getting Things Done - The Art of Stress-Free Productivity*. He recommends that you need to capture the essential elements necessary for you to get things done. Then, keep it out of your head in a reliable system where you can review it at any time.

Everything here includes what you have to do soon or someday (the big things and the small things). Some may be part of your work, while others may be part of your personal life. However, they should be the ones you regard as the most important and the ones you consider as less important.

Here are six reasons why you need to include everything:

- All things require your steady and conscious attention.

- You waste time and incur stress when you think of the same things repeatedly. Once you put them into a trusted system and out of your mind, you do them effortlessly.
- You have clarity on the number of things you need to do
- Since you are not distracted by indefinite stuff in your mind, your concentration increases.
- You can reject the things you shouldn't, and don't want to do since you have a clear idea of your commitments.
- You can start using your mind for creative activities rather than trying to remember things.

2. Be decisive

"When there is no next action; there is an infinite gap between current reality and what has to be done." - David Allen

Change is inevitable whether we like it or not. Hence, you need the discipline to decide the next best course of action. You must have a clear idea about your commitment to each activity. Then, make a decision about such a thing.

For your organization to work smoothly, you must empty your inbox regularly. Define and clarify each thing you have captured previously. Also, you need to decide what you will do with each item. What are your reasons for doing it?

When you know your reasons, you:

- You become aware of the reality and focus on the essential things rather than being carried away by what's urgent. Thus, your anxiety levels are at the barest minimum
- Are in full control because you know what to do and when to do it

- Experience a feeling of relief each time you make a decision. Also, you are not under any intense pressure since you have a clearer perspective about your goals
- Have higher self-esteem since you are responsible for your actions
- Are more productive since you have a reinforced ability to get things done.

3. Update your system regularly

"You have train yourself to see the forest and the tree before your knowledge can be productive" - Peter F. Drucker

You need to review your system regularly to make it useful. Reflect on the essential things in your life, work, current projects, and next actions frequently. Here are a few crucial reasons why you need to review your system regularly:

- A complete review reveals what you are not doing that you should be doing
- Since each action has a clearly defined step, missing one step would affect your result.

Essential Rules for Successful Time Management

It is an open secret that effective time management has loads of benefits. How many times have you heard that better time management reduces stress, saves time, and boosts efficiency? I am sure it's more than you can count. But the truth is, we often struggle to practice effective time management

We procrastinate, then, when we realize that the deadline is close, we start rushing to meet with the timeline. No one has the power to slow downtime, but you can get the most of your day by managing your time correctly.

Here are some proven time management tips to become a master of time management:

1. Batch them together

Batch related work together. For example, schedule a specific period to answer your emails and phone calls. Don't handle these tasks or similar tasks throughout the day. Different projects require a different thought process. Hence, batching together related tasks prevents your brain from switching to different thought processes each time you have to accomplish a different job. Batching helps your mind to eliminate the time it takes for your brain to reorient to accommodate the different new task.

2. Focus on the important aspects

This tip is a credit to Leo Babauta of the Zen Habits blog. According to him, you have to spend a few minutes to understand what needs to be done then, focus on those crucial things alone. Thus, you make every action count and create more value. In this case, less is not more; less is better.

3. Telecommute

Based on research, the average American commutes for at least 25 minutes. It is even predicted that this average time will increase in the nearest future. Add this time to the time it takes you to be prepared for your commute. Then, you will discover that you are wasting considerable time going to and coming back from work. The solution: if it's remotely possible with your job, try telecommuting at least once per week. You will save several hours per week which you can use for other productive means.

4. Make the best of your wait time

By all standards, I'm a patient person. But I can't stand waiting knowing I can spend that time more productively. Hence, I think of the best ways to spend that time. For example, if I'm waiting to see my doctor, I could create a blueprint for an upcoming blog post, listen to a podcast, or read an inspirational book.

5. Incorporate support habits

Charles Duhigg wrote a book called *The Power of Habits,* where he defined keystone habits. These life-transforming habits include meditating, developing daily routines, tracking what you eat, and exercising. By incorporating these support habits into your daily routine, you will replace bad habits with good habits over time. Consequently, you are more focused, healthier, and a better manager of your time.

6. Don't be afraid to say "No."

While you don't want your colleagues to be angry with you, you have limited time just like everyone else. For example, if you don't have spare time, you shouldn't try helping your colleagues with their assigned tasks.

7. Maximize the use of Google Calendar

Though calendars have been a fundamental time management tool for a long time, online calendars have taken it to the next level. You can access an online calendar from multiple devices. Then, use that tool to schedule recurring events, create time blocks, set up reminders, easily schedule meetings, and appointments.

While I think Google Calendar is the best because it's the one I use, Apple Calendar and Outlook can serve the same purpose.

8. Schedule buffer time between tasks or meetings

It may seem like a good use of your time to jump to a new project immediately after completing a previous task. But it has an opposite effect; it clutters your mind. The human brain can only focus for at least 90 minutes at once.

Hence, you need time even if it's a few minutes to recharge your mind, refresh your body, and boost your brain. Walking and meditation are two proven ways to clear your mind and recharge. Otherwise, you will struggle to focus or stay motivated. Based on my experience, a buffer time of 25 minutes between tasks is always ideal.

9. Alter your schedule

Altering your schedule can be a simple and effective solution to your time management struggles. For example, you can wake one hour earlier than your usual time. You can use this extra hour to work on side projects, check your emails, plan your day, exercise, or a combination of these tasks. Also, consider cutting down the amount of TV you watch and maintain the same wake-up routines during weekends.

10. Stop half-work.

According to James Clear, author of the *New York Times* best-seller *Atomic Habits*: "In this age of constant distraction, it's easy to split our focus between societal demands and what we should do. Typically, we are trying to accomplish a task and at the same time checking our to-do lists, emails, and messages. Hence, we can't fully focus on the project we are trying to accomplish."

Here some of the examples he gave of what he called "half-work":

- Your mind is wandering to your email inbox while communicating on the phone

- Writing a report, then, stopping to check your phone for no reason
- Altering your workout routine because you watched a couple of YouTube videos

The point is, when you engage in half-work, it takes you twice the time to accomplish a task, and you will only achieve half the mission. Clear opined that the best solution to half-work is to focus on one project and complete it before thinking about or starting any other task.

For example, pick an exercise and focus on it alone for your workouts. Also, leave your phone in a separate room and devote a significant amount of time on a substantial project. Clear claims that "the best way to achieve deep, focused work and avoid half-work is to eliminate distractions."

11. List all measurable steps to complete a task

All goals and projects are a sum of small moving parts. Hence, you need to clearly define the small moving parts to accomplish a project or goal. A side benefit is that you are motivated by what you have achieved. Thus, you can become focused on what you're yet to accomplish.

When you experience interruptions, ensure you are not entirely carried away by the distraction. A proven way to avoid getting taken away by a distraction is to limit the number of tasks you are performing at a specific time.

12. Apply the Eisenhower principle

You need to identify the urgent and essential tasks from your to-do list before working on them. This concept was first coined by Dwight D. Eisenhower, the 34th US president.

- You achieve personal goals with important tasks

- You achieve immediate goals with urgent tasks. Typically, urgent tasks have immediate consequences but are associated with accomplishing another person's intent.

Eisenhower's principle suggests prioritizing tasks into four groups:

- Not urgent and not important: These are complete distractions. Avoid them.
- Urgent but not important: these are barriers to your tasks, and your co-workers mostly provide them. They seek your help to accomplish their tasks. When this happens, you can suggest another competent person for them or say "No."
- Not urgent but important: These are tasks necessary to accomplish your goals. Thus, ensure you properly prepare for them.
- Urgent and important: These are the first tasks you should undertake every day. Some might be last-minute tasks, while others might be emergency tasks. With proper planning, you can prevent last-minute tasks. But you can't plan for emergency issues. Your best option is to allow a buffer time to deal with such problems. Including time slots for emergencies is one of the best ways to prioritize your tasks.

13. Apply the concept of leverage to complete your task

The smart use of leverage will help you to achieve the most significant returns with the least effort. Use the Pomodoro technique to avoid working overtime. This technique suggests that you "divide and structure your work into 25-minute sessions and a 5-minute break between the sessions."

For example, assuming you're working on a presentation and you've estimated that you need about 150 minutes to accomplish the task. Divide the task into six 25-minute sessions and a 5-minute break between them. Ensure that your sessions are not in conflict with other commitments or plans. Start working once the timer sets off after 25 minutes. Rest for 5 minutes after each session, then, repeat till you complete the sessions. Rest for 30 minutes after completing all the sessions.

14. Track your time
I have saved the best for the last. The first step to proper time management is to determine how you spend your time. You may believe you spend just 25 minutes on emails, while in reality, you spend more than 45 minutes on it per day.

Time apps such as my app calendar, Toggl, or RescueTime offers an easy way for you to track your time and activities weekly. Track your activities for next week, then, use the report to identify your time stealers and make appropriate adjustments.

5 Lesser-Known Productivity Hacks You Need to Know

As a live, breathing human being, there are times you will struggle with your productivity. Often, our inability to produce results consistently and repeatedly is one major thing that holds us back in life. For most of us, there are times we have peak productivity, but most times we have valley productivity. These are the main barriers to our life goals.

Before you can make significant progress in life, you must be productive consistently and repeatedly. You can't have five days of valley productivity and two days of high productivity in any given week. At the very least, you should have five days of high productivity and two days of valley productivity in any given week. However, we all struggle to be highly productive at all times.

Sometimes, we are on high productivity alert. At other times, something zaps our spirit, and our productivity declines. We either indulge in one of our preferred pleasures, or we hit one of life's stumbling blocks. Consequently, our relationships, health, careers, and finances suffer.

What's the solution?

First, you need to identify the impediments to your productivity. Examples of such obstacles include the inability to focus, lack of focus, poor time management skills, and procrastination. If you desire any significant, positive changes in your life, you must learn how to overcome these impediments consistently.

What are productivity hacks?
Hacks are tricks, skills, or shortcuts that can improve your productivity. Bear in mind there are no new productivity hacks; there are only multiple workarounds for us to get and stay productive.

Here are the best five of such hacks:

1. Focus on small and fast wins
Trying to do many things all at once is a common mistake. Another usual error is taking on a huge project in one go. If you want to get things done, start by taking baby steps one at a time.

Split your most important goal into:

- Daily goals
- Weekly goals
- Monthly goals
- Quarterly goals
- Yearly goals

Then, always ask yourself: "What's that one step I will take today that will make me closer to my end goal?" Focus on small and fast wins; avoid dreaming about your big goal.

These small and fast wins will help you to achieve your big goal over time.

Example; big goal: Become a self-published author.

Since a typical book has about 300 pages, you need to a little over 75,000 words (an average of 250 words per page) for the 300 pages.

Breakdown: make it a habit to write 400 words per day rather than thinking about the end goal (75,000 words). Start with 100 words today, and by the end of next week, you must have written another 1,000 words. If you continue that way, you should complete your 300-page book within six months.

That's the magic that happens when you focus on small and fast wins.

2. Don't break the consistency
If you are trying to build a habit within 21 days because you read it or watched it somewhere, you are wrong. The truth is, it takes between 18 and 254 days to build a habit. The key to forming any pattern is consistency. A strong start but giving up too soon is one primary reason why most people are unable to build life-changing habits. If you fall into this category, then, apply the Jerry Seinfeld productivity hack. It's also known as the "don't break the chain" hack.

Here's an excerpt from an article on life hacker by Brad Isaac in which Jerry Seinfeld explains this hack:

"The best way to be the best comic is to create better jokes. Writing every day is the way to create better jokes. Use a unique calendar system as a leverage technique to pressure yourself to write. Get a wall calendar with a whole year on one page and hang it where it can be prominent. Then, use a big red magic marker to put a big red x over each day you perform your task. You should have a chain after a few days of consistent practice. The chain will keep growing, provided you keep at it. After a few weeks of consistency, you will be motivated to keep the chain growing. Thus, your only task is to avoid breaking the chain."

This hack is useful because it helps you to be consistent with your skill or talent.

The three steps to get started with this hack:

Step 1: Figure out your skill or learn it. You can choose to become a master at SEO, a highly sought-after programmer or an exceptional stand-up comedian. This is a vital step; don't skip it.

Step 2: Put up a one-year calendar on a prominent space in your home, office, or workplace.

Step 3: As you devote time to work on that skill, cross each day with a big x. Focus on lengthening the chain. Your only task is to avoid breaking the chain.

3. Use a standing desk

I know it seems crazy, but using a standing desk can improve your focus and productivity by up to 46%. New evidence by Texas A & M University research suggests that employees using standing desks are 46% more productive than those using the traditional seated desk configurations. Now, most hip office use standing desks. Also, FF Venture capital discovered that results in more active sharing of ideas. It is a well-known fact Thomas Jefferson, and a few other prominent individuals worked at standing desks for most days of their lives.

Other benefits of working at a standing desk at home or workplace include:

- Increased productivity. You won't check your inbox too frequently
- Calorie reduction. Using a standing desk exercises the significant muscles in your legs
- Improved focus. It is normal to feel a sense of urgency when standing. Thus, you are more focused and can complete tasks on time
- Improvements to your digestive health. A standing desk prevents you from sleeping at your desk. Thus, you experience less fatigue.

When you use standing desks, you have little or no urge to multitask, switch between websites, check email, and be distracted in any other way.

How to get started:
- **Start in small cycles.** Rather than start working at your standing desk for straight hours. Start with baby steps. Start with 20 minutes per day, then increase this time gradually till you can ultimately spend your day on a standing desk
- **Use Pinterest** or similar sites to get creative ideas on setting up your standing desk
- **Take breaks.** Avoid stiffness or fatigue by consuming a cup of coffee, practicing squats or going for a short walk.

4. Implement the 2-minute rule

It is surprising to know that you can accomplish quite a lot within two minutes. The inclusion of mundane tasks in a daily to-do list is one of the reasons why 90% of people never achieve the tasks on their to-do lists. Thus, you need a systemic approach to tackling your to-do list. That systemic approach is the 2-minute rule.

By implementing the 2-minute rule, you focus on essential tasks and eliminate the unimportant tasks.

The 2-minute rule is split into two parts:

- Start and complete anything that can be accomplished within two minutes
- Start anything that takes more than two minutes to accomplish

Part 1. Start and complete anything that can be accomplished within two minutes

Don't add this 2-minute task to your to-do list, don't procrastinate about it and don't outsource it. Do it immediately and forget about it. Tasks that fit into a 2-minute project include cleaning up clutter, sending that email, taking out the garbage, tossing the laundry in the washing machine, washing your dishes immediately after your meal.

With time, you will start uncovering more 2-minute tasks. Build and maintain excitement in your workday by ticking off this 2-minute task. There's a sense of accomplishment synonymous with getting things done. By micro-managing unimportant tasks through the 2-minute principle, you can manage your daily to-do lists with greater effectiveness.

Part 2. Start anything that takes more than two minutes to accomplish

If you have 2-hour, 2-day, 2-week, or 2-month tasks, then, you may start wondering how to accomplish them down within two minutes. When you build momentum by accomplishing a 2-minute task, you feel better equipped to perform more significant tasks. This is one primary reason why the 2-minute rule is quite potent.

Examples of tasks you can turn into a 2-minutes project include:

- "Run three miles," is now "Tie my running shoes."
- "Fold the laundry" becomes "Fold one pair of socks."
- "Study for class" turns to "Open my notes."
- "Do 20 minutes of yoga" starts with "Take out my yoga mat."
- "Read before bed each night" becomes "Read one page."

You set the precedence to move onto more significant tasks by using the 2-minute rule to take immediate action on your goals.

5. Miscellaneous hacks

   1. ***When browsing with Google Chrome***
      - **Pin websites to desktop**

If you visit some websites regularly, pin them to your desktop as apps. To do this, open the website you want to pin, go to Chrome settings, more tools, then, click on "create shortcut."

   - **Use these popular Chrome shortcuts**
      - Ctrl+shift+n: opening a new window in incognito mode
      - Ctrl+j: open "recent downloads"
      - Shift+esc: Opens Google Chrome's task manager
      - Alt+enter: open URL in a new tab after typing the URL manually

- Ctrl/shift+f5: reload the current page while ignoring cached content

2. *Do this last thing each night but the first thing each morning*
Send yourself an email before you sleep. This email should contain your top three goals for the next day. This is an often-overlooked productivity hack, yet it is straightforward.

Most times, you may have forgotten what you even wrote, probably because of stress, exhaustion, or a good night's sleep.

Chapter 3 - A Guide to Goal-Setting

All About the Goal-Setting Theory of Motivation

Edwin Locke proposed the goal-setting theory of motivation in the 1960s. This theory states that goal setting hugely depends on task performance. It says that specific, challenging goals with appropriate feedback results in higher and better task performance.

Goals indicate and guide the employee on the task to be achieved and the number of efforts required to accomplish it.

The efficiency of the goal depends on the type and quality of the goal.

Imagine you are 40 pounds overweight and need to drop the extra weight. Here are some options you have when setting the goal:

- "I want to shed the extra pounds before this time next year. I will review my diet and make appropriate recommendations." This goal isn't specific and lacks clarity. You need to specify the amount of weight you want to lose within that period and the particular steps to shedding this extra weight.
- "I will lose two pounds a week over the next four months. My exercise routine will be 40 minutes per day, five days a week. Also, I will include whole-grain products, vegetables, and three fruit servings in my diet. Lastly, I won't eat out at all for the next month. Then, I will only eat out once per week after the next month." This is a more specific and more clearly-defined goal than the previous one.

The principal motivation is the willingness to work towards achieving the set goal. Easy, general, and vague goals are less motivating than clear, specific, and challenging goals.

Goal-Setting Principles

Based on his research in 1968, Dr. Edwin Locke published an article titled, *'Towards a theory of task motivation and incentives."* In this article, he provided proof that a clearly-defined goal with proper feedback motivates people to accomplish their goals. He also opined that the thrills involved in achieving a goal is a motivation in itself and improves performance. Summarily, Locke suggests that we tend to work harder to attain specific and challenging goals, especially in a work environment.

Years later, Dr. Gary Latham conducted his goal setting research in a work environment. Like Locke, he aimed to establish the correlation between setting goals and employee performance in the workplace.

In 1990, Locke and Latham jointly published their most famous work, *"A theory of goal setting & task performance."* The published work emphasized the importance of setting a specific and challenging goal. They also developed five basic principles responsible for success in goal setting.

Goals should:

- Be clear. A clearly-defined goal is more achievable than a poorly-defined one. Goals with a specific timeline of completion are usually the most effective.
- Be challenging. A goal with a slight level of difficulty will provide you with the motivation to accomplish the goal
- Involve a level of commitment. When you are committed to your goal, you will make the necessary effort to achieve the

goal. Also, being accountable can increase your level of commitment towards the goal. One simple and effective way to be responsible is to share your goal with a friend, relative, or trusted colleague.
- Have appropriate feedback. However, there has to be proper feedback to improve performance towards achieving the next goal. Feedback is the tool to regulate goal difficulties, make clarifications, and gain reputation. In a work environment, feedback helps the employee to be more involved in attaining the next goal. Hence, they become more satisfied with their job.
- Include the time for overcoming the learning curve. This is especially true for complex projects. Thus, having the time to master the learning curve gives you the best chance of success.

When employees are involved in setting the goal, they are more receptive towards the goal and are more involved in attaining the goal.

The goal-setting theory makes two specific assumptions:

Assumption #1: Goal Commitment

The goal-setting theory assumes that the individual will not abandon the goal because he's fully committed to it. However, you can only be committed to a goal when:

- It is open, accessible and the widespread
- You are not assigned the goal, but you are the one setting the goal
- Your set goal is consistent with your corporation; s goals and vision

Assumption #2: Self-Efficiency

This is your self-confidence and faith in performing the task. Your level of self-efficiency will determine the amount of effort you will apply when struggling with any aspect of the project. The reverse is also true; if your level of self-efficiency becomes too low, you may even quit before accomplishing the task.

How to Apply the Goal-Setting Theory in Your Life
Carefully consider the goals you set when trying to improve an aspect of your daily life. Ensure that each task obeys the goal-setting principles discussed above.

Ensure you set goals that are suitable to one's abilities. For example, you could help your child succeed academically by allowing her to set the goal. For example, assume she wants to get 100% in her next English test. Not only is she committed to this goal, but the goal is also clear and challenging.

Now, you only need to discuss whether or not the goal is attainable. If she typically gets Cs in English assignments, it might be a poor goal to achieve a perfect score at the next attempt. Then, you need to develop specific steps towards achieving the goal. You also need to consider the amount of time required to achieve the objective and the complexity involved.

Ultimately, her goal might be: "I want a 100% score in my English test. I will start practicing neat and clean handwriting, then, learn how to use the appropriate words. My dad will give me feedback on how to fix my mistakes." Now, this is a specific plan to receive proper feedback because it is a clear, achievable goal, and she has the right motivation to achieve it. According to the goal-setting theory, she will perform better in her next test even if she couldn't obtain 100% on it.

The only limitation to the goal-setting theory is that it can fail when you lack the skill and competence to perform necessary actions towards achieving the goal.

Bear these principles in mind when next you want to determine your (individual or team) goals:

1. *Set clear and precise goals*

A clear goal is measurable and is devoid of understanding. The desired outcome will determine the explicitness of the objective and how it will be measured. Synonymous with the SMART goal-setting principle, clear goals should improve the understanding of the task, make results measurable and success inevitable. Consider how you will measure results. Does your goal excite you? Is it challenging enough? As you think about it, do you feel the motivation to complete it? If you answered negatively to any of these questions, you might have to reconsider this goal.

Clear goal:

- Implement technology to reduce product development time from 20 minutes to 15 minutes by the end of the year
- I want to lose 15 pounds in 2 months

Unclear goal:

- Decrease product development time
- I want to lose weight

When your goal is concrete and measurable, achieving it becomes easily possible, and you can easily track your progress.

2. Make your goals challenging

"A goal that inspires your hopes, liberates your energy and commands your thoughts will make you happy." - Andrew Carnegie.

To ensure you have the right degree of challenge, setting challenging goals requires a considerable balance. Your motivation and performance depend on the simplicity or difficulty in achieving the goal. You reach the highest level of motivation when your goal lies between difficult and easy.

The next time you set goals, make sure they are trying but attainable, challenging, but realistic. Here are a few questions you can ask yourself when setting your goals:

- Are they realistic and achievable?
- Do they provide enough motivation?
- Do they give enough challenge?

Challenging:

- Convert 65% more prospects to clients in Q3 FY 2018-19 compared with 45% Q2 FY 2018-19.
- Lose 40 pounds within two months

Easily achievable:

- Convert 1% more prospects to clients in Q3 FY 2018-19 compared to Q2 FY 2018-19.
- Lose 1 pound within two months

Your goal should be difficult enough to make you feel accomplished.

3. *Truly and genuinely commit to your goals*

You must fully understand and agree to your goals, whether you are setting the goal for yourself, your employees, or teammates before you can accomplish such goals. Mostly, when working in a team, your teammates will more likely work harder for the objective provided they have been involved in setting the goal. You shouldn't have any motivation problem till the goal is accomplished, provided the goal is achievable and consistent with the aspirations of all your teammates.

Imagine the tasks you accomplish daily at work; which ones do you exert the most effort and which ones do you perform without interest or enthusiasm. Your motivation to achieve your goals depends on your emotional commitment to the objective.

Correct: Project manager and his team decide the expected outcome of a meeting subject to each teammate's talent and skills.

Incorrect: Project manager does not consider his team's bandwidth and capabilities before assigning goals to each of them.

4. *Obtain feedback on your progress*

"Goal setting becomes hugely effective when you have feedback that shows progress relative to the intended goal" - Prof. Edwin Locke

Once you've chosen the right goal, you should obtain feedback to determine your level of progress. Thus, you can decide whether to adjust the goal or adjust your approach to attain the goal. Feedback can be self-adjudged, but it usually comes from other people.

Correct:

- Perform weekly checks on the design department to monitor their progress. Provide feedback on whether they need to alter the process, or they are on track.
- Tweak weight loss routine after losing one pound in two weeks

Incorrect:

- Set and forget about a task. When the deadline approaches, start getting anxious about completing the task.
- Wait after two months before tracking any changes

Frequently set aside some time to review your goals and track your progress. Thus, you are motivated continuously through the process of achieving your goal.

5. *Simplify complex tasks*

Be careful not to complicate your goals. When your objectives become too complicated, it negatively affects your motivation, productivity, and morale. Most people become overwhelmed when goals become highly complex. When you have complex goals, allow enough time to learn (when necessary), practice and improve performance until the goal is achieved. When necessary, modify the goal by reassessing its complexity or difficulty. You can also break those goals into smaller sub-goals.

Bear in mind that nothing worth its salt will ever be easily accomplished. But using simpler, less-complicated sub-tasks can help you to break down and overcome daunting tasks.

Remember that *"the journey of a thousand miles starts with taking the first step"* - Lao Tzu

Correct: Break down and distribute target sales among all salespeople, depending on their abilities. Thus, the entire target sales can be achieved within a specific period.

Incorrect: Expect one salesperson to achieve the entire target sales within a specific period

You need to keep working at your goal setting, just like every other aspect of your life. Use the principles to implement your life goals, and you will be surprised at the greatness you will achieve.

15 of the Best Tips for Effective Goal-Setting

You're virtually guaranteed success when you are clear about your life's purpose. You can determine your vision, convert your desires into achievable goals, and act on them.

My past experiences have taught me that being selective about my new year's goals, and thinking of ways to accomplish them has been hugely helpful. Goal setting is one proven way to transform impressive resolutions into actual results. Research shows that we are more likely to achieve our goals provided they are measurable.

When you have finished reading this section, you should have proven tips you can use to set your goals with greater efficiency:

1. **Make it physical.** Write down or type out your goals and action plans on paper. As you write them down, you will be more inclined to flesh them out. Thus, your action plans will not just be an outline. It will be a detailed roadmap you can follow.
2. **Regular review is key.** You should ensure that you review your goals at least once in a month, if not once a week. You

can schedule an appointment with yourself, a team member, a trusted colleague, or relative for the review. Hence, you can track your level of progress easily. I review my yearly goals every week to ensure I'm on the right track of progress towards my goal.
3. **Challenge yourself without being stupid.** While it is good to choose goals that will excite and stretch you, you must also ensure that these goals are attainable. Thus, you can truly measure your progress over a specific period. The idea is to accomplish the goals and have something valuable you can celebrate at the end of the year. If you constantly have unachievable goals or white elephant projects, you start developing a habit of failure.
4. **Be exact with your action plans.** Write down the exact steps that can help you to accomplish your goal. For example, you need to show your business plan to potential investors when starting a business before they can take you seriously.
5. **Quality is always better than quantity.** Rather than having a long wish list of tasks which you may never accomplish, why not have three or four solid goals? Once you've accomplished the most important goals, you can add more goals later.
6. **Be specific.** For example: create a blog with 10,000 monthly visitors is more specific than creating a blog with thousands of monthly visitors. Similarly, "gaining 1,500 Twitter followers" is more specific than "having a strong social media presence."
7. **Deadlines make concrete goals.** Your action plan is incomplete without a timeline to achieve the goal. Break down your big goal to smaller sub-goals. Then, set deadlines for these sub-goals till you attain the big goal.
8. **Accountability is important.** Share your goals with a friend or a loved one. They will make you accountable for achieving

your goal. The law of commitment states that "When we tell others what we intend to accomplish, we have a natural tendency to remain committed till we achieve it." Thus, you have the needed impetus to take all the necessary steps until you can attain your goal.

9. **Make it obvious.** Tape your goals where they are pronounced. This place can be your door fridge or your bathroom mirror. If you stick it in a drawer, you will forget about it, and it won't do you any good. The idea here is to maintain top of mind awareness. You will easily forget what's not on top of your mind. Another way to keep your goals top of mind is to read your goals every day.

10. **Maintain flexibility.** When you have to scale back, recalibrate, or revise to take care of emergencies, ensure that these changes move you forward. This is one benefit of having a monthly review of your yearly goals.

11. **Love and appreciate the process.** The results you desire and the goal-setting process to achieve the goal are equally important. If you constantly think about what you're yet to achieve, you won't appreciate the process or the sub-goals you've already achieved. When you appreciate and honor the adventure, you will remain positive, confident, and motivated.

12. **Use the rule of 5.** The rule of 5 ensures that you take daily steps towards attaining your goals. Identify and accomplish five specific steps that will get you closer to your goal. These steps don't have to be big. Sending an email or making a quick call is fine provided they are relevant to your goal. But quit for the day until you complete these five steps. Thus, you have a proven structure to maximize your day and give you a clarity of what you can achieve daily. If you use this rule and stick with it, you can make consistent progress without exhausting

yourself. Where necessary, you can scale back your goals or round them up.
13. **Don't neglect self-care.** If you're malnourished, overworked, or stressed, you may never attain your goals. If you do, you may suffer ill-health as a result of the stress and overwork. While achieving your dreams, don't neglect self-care. Your body will thank you, and you will preserve your health and sanity.
14. **Keep score.** Why do you check the score immediately you tune into a sports station? You want to know which team is winning and how long for them to hold on. You should also be keeping score with the goals you've set. I suggest you use a physical chart. Identify the goal and outline the steps you need to achieve this goal. Track your progress and for every success, reward yourself. Using visual charts will show you that you are avoiding any shortcuts.
15. **Never give up.** If you don't give up but implement the tips above, you will succeed and achieve your goals even faster.

8 Common Reasons Why To-Do Lists Fail

Most people using to-do lists struggle to cross-out every item on the list by the time they are off to bed in the night. Even the tasks completed aren't part of the to-do lists. If to-do lists don't work for you, they would seem to be highly ineffective. You may be killing your productivity with your to-do lists. This section reveals why your to-do lists fail and what you can do about it.

   1. **You're allowing energy vampires**

These are self-centered people who sap your energy without considering your time and priorities. They are the ones continually seeking your help over one task or the other. Most times, these are time-consuming tasks that are neither beneficial to you or on your to-do list.

If the energy vampire is a work colleague, you can send him this simple message. "I'm under a tight deadline now, and unfortunately, I can't help out at the moment." If this colleague remains persistent, send him a message similar to the one below: "I'm currently working on [state your current task here]. But I can loop in my supervisor and ask him how to prioritize."

2. You're writing your to-do list in the morning

Write your to-do list before going to bed. Thus, you avoid wasting your energized morning mojo to develop your daily tasks. A side benefit of creating your to-do list before going to bed is that it calms your mind. Psychiatrists and psychologists even recommend this technique to avoid anxiety. Keep out unwanted thoughts by establishing a plan for your next 24-hours. You won't disturb your sleep with thoughts of "you have a parent meeting at 2 pm" or "you must finish the report by 6 pm tomorrow."

3. Your to-do list has too many items

Out of 6,500 LinkedIn professionals, only 11% of them finish their to-do tasks by the end of the day. When you have too many items on your to-do list, you are setting yourself up for failure. Also, you deprive yourself of that end-of-day excitement of accomplishing your daily task. Also, when your to-do list is too much, it becomes highly discouraging. You will be more inclined to procrastinate since you won't know where to start.

Choosing at most three most important tasks is one effective way I've found to improve my productivity and manage my time correctly.

Your most important tasks are measurable, generative, have meaning when completed, and move you towards accomplishing your goals.

4. You don't create time for urgent distractions

After making all the efforts to understand and write down your priorities. An email from a co-worker or a piece of breaking news is all it takes to distract you. So, you're off track the moment you receive your first urgent message despite all your productivity efforts.

A simple and effective solution is to create space in your schedule without any task. Thus, you have space to accommodate emergencies. Then, on days where there are no emergencies, you finish your day early and take the rest of the day off. You can also take proactive measures to avoid distractions. Adjust your email settings only to receive messages from specific people, set your phone calls to voicemails and make your status "busy" on private chats.

5. Your to-do list lack specificity

In an interview with Bloomberg Business, David Allen said, "Ninety-nine percent of every to-do list I have seen is an incomplete list of unclear stuff. You will see things like 'bank,' 'doctor,' or 'mom.' While these may look good, you need to include an action step with it." Instead of 'bank,' write down the specific task such as 'create a new savings account at the bank'."

6. You're not sorting your to-do list

After identifying your three most important tasks for the day, classify other goals into:

- A long-term list
- A weekly list.

Your long-term list should contain your 3-month or 6-month goal. For example, "completely cut out all unnecessary expenses." the weekly to-do list for this 6-month goal would be: "Stop eating out for the next X weeks."

7. Your to-do list lacks a deadline

There is no difference between a wish list and a to-do list without deadlines. Deadlines tilt us towards taking action. Where there are no deadlines, you lack the motivation to take action. This is one reason why your to-do list keeps growing without finishing most of the tasks on the list.

When you set deadlines, you prioritize tasks or projects to complete them within a specified timeframe. Remember Parkinson's law: *"Work expands to fill the time available for its completion."* You need to assign deadlines to your to-do items. Otherwise, don't be surprised that you can't finish most of the tasks.

8. You don't understand why you need a to-do list

For most people, when you ask them the basis for creating a to-do list, their answer is always: "to get things done." However, that's the wrong reason for creating a properly-designed to-do list. The primary purpose of a to-do list is to organize and highlight your most important tasks. By writing them down, you gain a panoramic view of your most essential duties.

A properly-designed to-do list should help you concentrate on the right work and avoid any distractions. Your task list is a tool to get the right things done; it's not a tool to get everything done. Reread the statement above again until you correctly understand the difference. When you misunderstand the role of your to-do list, you will create and use an ineffective one. Thus, rather than increase your productivity, you end up restricting it.

Time Management

Now you have a to-do list approach that can make your day rather than break it. Note that you should write this long-term and weekly to-do list on a separate page in your journal.

Chapter 4 - The Secrets of Productivity

How to Prioritize When Everything Is Important

You're not alone; we all don't enough time to do everything we want to do. However, does everything on your to-do list feel important (or your superior feels that way)? Then, it's time for you to implement any of the prioritization techniques in this section. Thus, your to-do list can become more manageable and conquerable.

What's a Prioritization Technique?
Which of the 150 tasks on your task list is the most important? The prioritization technique will help you to answer this question correctly. This technique provides you with a formal method to evaluate the importance of finishing each task on your list. By implementing the prioritization process, you can make the right decisions about the project you need to do. But delete the ones that are less urgent and less important. You can even specify a period for a particular task.

The prioritization techniques solve two vital issues:

Issue #1: Do you feel you've spent all your day performing urgent tasks for everyone who've sought your help? Then, a prioritized list will help you to avoid unreasonable last-minute panic assignments and regain control of your time.

Issue #2: Are those meeting requests or incoming emails that important? You'll never complete important work when you allow other people to create your to-do list for you through incoming emails and meeting requests. When you know the specific tasks to focus on and the reason to focus on that task, you can easily justify delaying answering that email or declining a meeting invite.

Time Management

During my time in a product development team, we often use our prioritized list to prevent distractions and delays. When stakeholders made new and urgent requests, we show them the prioritized list. Then, ask, "Which task should we remove to accommodate your new request?" Often, once they see the importance of the other items on the list, their urgent requests suddenly become less urgent.

You can also use this technique to manage priorities with your family, co-workers, and your boss. It can also work for that part of your brain that's always searching for new ideas, giving you reasons to procrastinate on valuable work.

Use these prioritization techniques to focus on your most important work. You have to choose the right prioritization technique that makes sense and works for you. Fortunately, you can find a method that works for you from any of these prioritization techniques:

1. **Priority Matrix**

This technique involves distributing your tasks into a 4-box array. The y-axis represents a value, while the x-axis represents another one. Then, each quadrant represents a priority defined by the values.

The image below illustrated this technique.

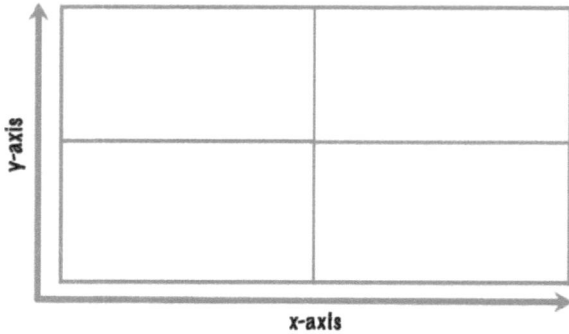

The Eisenhower matrix is a famous example of a priority matrix. In this matrix, urgency is the x-axis value, while importance is the y-axis value. Use urgency and importance to evaluate tasks, before placing each task in the correct quadrant. Thus, the Eisenhower matrix looks like the image below:

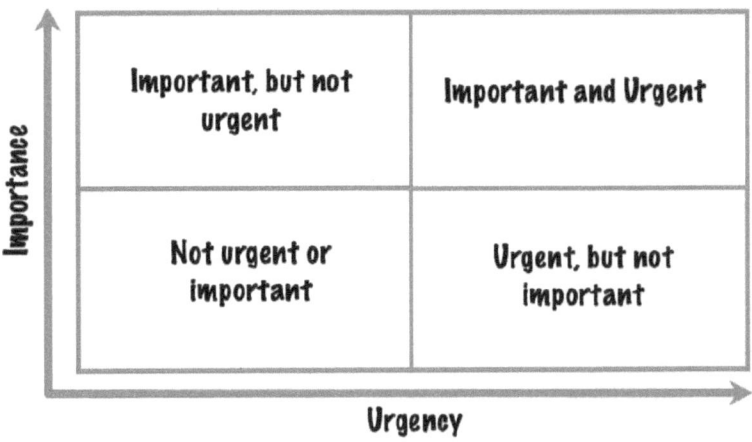

After placing each task in its suitable quadrant, you can determine what you need to delete from your list. You can also uncover what you need to delegate, what you need to work on later, and what you need to work on now.

Note that you can use any values that make sense to you as your x-and y-axis values in the priority matrix.

Here are two additional examples:

a. Effort-impact matrix

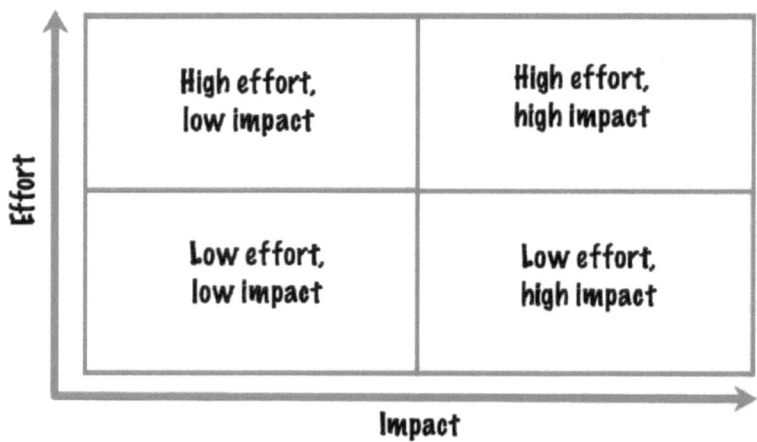

In this matrix, you assess tasks based on the effort you will exert to complete them and the impact of completing them. Your priorities are the tasks in the two right-side quadrants. Since the "low effort, high impact" tasks represent quick wins; they are likely your highest priorities.

b. Value-cost matrix

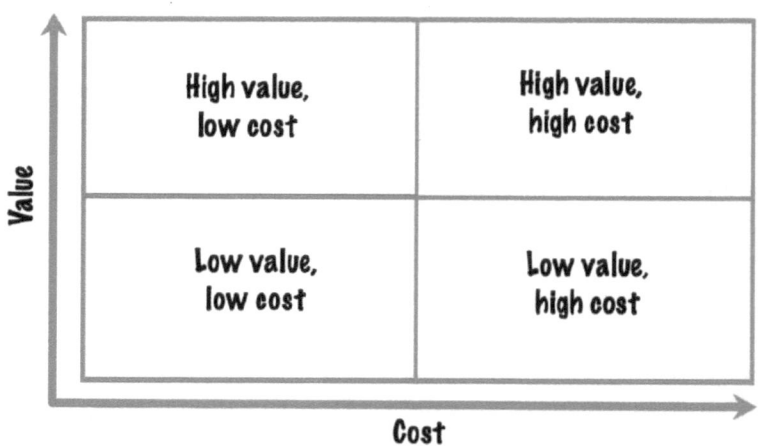

In this matrix, your priorities are the top two quadrants. Your quick wins are the "high value, low cost" tasks, but you should avoid executing "low value, high cost" tasks. If the priority matrix resonates with you, you can build your matrices in a spreadsheet, on paper, use the priority matrix app or the free Eisenhower matrix app.

2. MoSCoW (pronounced just like Russia's capital city)

In this simple prioritization technique, you categorize every task on your to-do list into four:

- M tasks-must do: Highly important tasks
- S tasks-should do: Though they are lower of a lower priority than m tasks, the s tasks are things you should do
- C tasks-could do: These are tasks you'd like to do. However, if you don't do them, it won't matter at all
- W tasks-won't do: These are tasks that aren't worth your time at all

How to use this technique

Use the MoSCoW to categorize each task. The order of priority of your tasks should be M, S, and C. Delete your W tasks.

Then, start working on your list from the top-down, and you can be sure that you're working on your highest-priority tasks.

Trello or any other Kanban app (available on Android and iTunes stores) is very useful for the MoSCoW method. Specify the order of each task by dragging and dropping them within the lists.

For optimal results with the MoSCoW method, ensure you add all your tasks to a master list before categorizing them. Use a zap (an automated Zapier workflow) to make this addition; it automates the movement of your mini-projects from Slack and your email inbox to your master to-do list.

3. ABCDE

A major demerit of the MoSCoW technique is that you can't use it for task delegation. The best alternative is to use Brian Tracy's ABCDE method (details in his "Eat The Frog" book). The ABCDE method is similar to the MoSCoW method.

- The A tasks are the M tasks in the MoSCoW method - do them
- The B tasks are the s tasks in the MoSCoW method
- The C tasks are the c tasks in the MoSCoW method
- The D tasks are tasks you should automate or delegate - this is the difference
- The E tasks are the w tasks in the MoSCoW method - delete them

Use the priority of each project to assign a letter to it. By delegating the D tasks and removing the E tasks, you can focus on the A, B, and C tasks - the most critical tasks.

You can also use Kanban apps for this technique. Your master list should sub-lists with A, B, C, D, and E tasks. Drag and drop tasks into the right category from the master list, then, start with your A tasks.

4. Agile Prioritization

This prioritization method, also known as scrum prioritization, relies on ordering your tasks. If you have 15 to-dos on your task list, use priority and sequence to arrange the mini-projects from 1-15. Scrum prioritization is highly effective when the series is highly essential. For example, assuming your most important task is to retile your bathroom floor, but they also have to run new pipes. Though running new pipes is a lower priority, it needs to be completed first because it will affect your most important task: retiling the floor.

There are three criteria for evaluating task in scrum prioritization:

- The importance of the project
- The significance of the project relative to other tasks
- Other projects that can affect this task

Assign each of these criteria a number 1 to N (N = total number of items on your list). Every item should have a unique number. No two tasks can be #1. Though scrum prioritization can be combined with the MoSCoW and ABCDE techniques, it's also useful on its own. Consider the inter-dependence of the tasks on one another before categorizing them by priority. Then, arrange them in order of completion.

Any drag-and-drop to-do list app is suitable for scrum prioritization. But for efficiency, rather than using drag and drop tools, you can use Yodiz (a scrum-specific tool) to assign numbers to each task. Yodiz has a free plan.

5. Bubble Sort

Let's rephrase criteria #2 of the scrum prioritization technique to "how important is a task relative to other tasks?" The bubble sort is a technique that compares the importance of tasks relative to one another. Hence, it's a useful technique for answering the question above. The first step to using this technique is to arrange all your to-do items on a horizontal grid:

| Task 1 | Task 2 | Task 3 | Task 4 | Task 5 | Task 6 |

Your next step is to compare the first two tasks and identify the most important one. Then, move the most critical item to the top left. Using the image above, assuming task 2 is more important than item 1, then, it becomes the first task of the horizontal grid.

Continue to compare the two closest tasks until you exhaust the list of tasks using the question above as the basis for rearranging the order of items.

After reordering the list completely, your least important priority is now to the far right, while your most important priority is now on the far left.

An example of a completely reordered list in order of priority is shown below:

| Task 2 | Task 1 | Task 6 | Task 4 | Task 3 | Task 5 |

Though there are no specific tools suitable for this technique, any project management app appropriate for drag-and-drop prioritization can work effectively. But instead of working on tasks from left-to-right, you work on them from top-to-bottom.

6. The 1-3-9 Technique

This technique allows you to prioritize urgent but less important tasks. Each day you are to complete 13 tasks:

- Nine low-importance items
- Three somewhat important tasks
- One crucial task

First, work and complete your one tasks, then, your three tasks and lastly, your nine tasks. The 1-3-9 method helps you to work on the most important of your less important tasks.

7. Two Lists

This technique is credited to Warren Buffet. Here's how it works: write down 25 to-do tasks, then, circle the top five items on this list. Next, group these tasks into two extensive lists. The first list which contains the five tasks you circled is now your to-do list. The second list which includes the other 20 items is now your don't do list. Complete all your five to-do tasks before spending any time on your don't do list. While you could accomplish this technique with any app that allows you to move tasks between lists, it is a technique designed to be performed on paper.

How to Choose Your Most Suitable Prioritization Technique

The goal of these prioritization techniques is the same - to help you work on your highest priority tasks. Hence, it doesn't matter whether you use one technique, multiple techniques, or combine parts of the different techniques. You must ensure that the technique you choose makes sense, feels natural, and is adequate for you.

The Chunking Technique for Making Your Goals Achievable

These days, we are pulled in a lot of directions on our personal and professional lives that the idea of free becomes an illusion. But imagine:

- You can bring higher efficiency to your life
- You can focus on achieving your goals rather than trying to accomplish an infinite number of tasks on your to-do lists

Imagine the free time it will open in your life and the positive change in the quality of your life. This desire to create free time is the basis of the rapid planning method (RPM). Apart from being a time management system, RPM helps you to focus on critical aspects that can help you to organize your life more efficiently. Thus, you can maximize your sense of fulfillment, joy, and optimize your desired outcomes. The assumption is that you are more driven to take actions that lead to your success when you have a clarity of purpose that drives your actions. Chunking (a highly efficient way to maximize your day) is one of the core components of RPM.

What is Chunking?
Chunking means arranging information into bit-sized pieces to produce your desired outcome without shutdown or stress. One source of stress in our lives is that we don't have enough time to do an infinite number of things for our lives. This strong emotion to get things done leads to the creation of to-do lists. But a large number of items on the list can lead to frustration. Thus, we won't even tackle any project on our list.

Based on my experience, three chunking methods have been the most effective:

- Chunk down by quantity
- Chunk down by the time
- Chunk down by actionable steps

Time Management

1. *Chunk down by quantity*

This means setting a quota. If you are a writer, you can set a quota for your writing. For example, you can write a maximum of 3 pages per day until you complete your novel.

Alternatively, your quota can be a word count. An example is a national novel writing month challenge. If you are a participant, you will be required to write 1,667 words per day, and by the end of the month, you would have completed a 50,000-word book.

Here are three other examples of chunking down a goal by quantity:

- Hit 300 balls daily to improve your tennis
- Learn ten French words per day for 100 days to improve your French fluency
- Do one drawing per day for one year to improve your drawing fluency

2. *Chunk down by the time*

A while back, I was overweight because I was making bad food choices, eating out a lot, and wasn't exercising. After choosing to shed some pounds, my nutritionist and I developed a plan for me to lose 30 pounds in three months. He provided me with a menu of what to eat during this month. I was also instructed to walk one hour daily.

Walking one hour per day became a significant component of chunking down my goal. Thus, I used the time to chunk down my goal of losing weight.

Here are some other goals that can be chunked down by time:

- Declutter for 10 minutes daily to be organized
- Practice piano for 40 minutes daily to become a master pianist

- Meditate for 15 minutes daily to manage stress

However, spending an hour per day to achieve my important goals remains my favorite way of chunking down my goals.

3. *Chunk down by actionable steps*

By creating a list of actionable steps, you can chunk down a goal you are not sure you could achieve. Goal, sub-goals, and actionable steps are three terms we would use to describe this method.

By definition,

- The goals are the target you intend to achieve
- Sub-goals are the milestones to achieve the goals
- Actionable steps are the single tasks to accomplish each sub-goal

Assuming you intend to "create a video course," but you've never created a course or made videos. Your first step is to establish a deadline for the video course creation. Let's use a 6-month (180-day) deadline. Next, open excel and create 180 spaces (a space for each day); this is your actionable steps list.

Now, create ten sub-goals to achieve your big goal. Anytime you need help with any creating the sub-goals, you can:

- talk to a video course creation expert,
- read a book about it,
- watch some YouTube videos, or perform online research.

For our video course creation example, here are ten sub-goals to achieve this goal:

- Suitable equipment
- Learning how to use the equipment

- Developing the title for the course
- Validate your title idea
- Develop your outline
- Develop the script
- Design the slides
- Start recording the videos
- Edit your videos (I recommend you outsource)
- Launch your course

To make things easy, let's assume each sub-goal has a deadline of 18 days (i.e., 180 days (the total deadline) divided by 10 (the number of sub-goals)). Thus, we need 18 actionable steps to achieve each sub-goal.

You can use the following guideline to create your actionable steps.

Actionable step for each day:

- One - what you can do right away to get started
- Two - the next physical action to take
- Repeat the steps above till you have actionable steps to complete your first sub-goal

If you complete a sub-goal in less 18 days, move to the next sub-goal. Then, continue until you accomplish your goal. As write down actionable steps, ask yourself this question: "Am I capable of taking the step immediately?" If your answer is "yes," then include this actionable step. Otherwise, break down this step further.

You can also use the CRUMBB technique, an acronym for "clearly realizable unit that's a meaningful building block." Realizable means you can take action immediately, while Meaningful means it moves you closer to complete your goal. You can read more about the

CRUMBB method in a book titled "master the moment" written by best-selling author, Pat Brans.

Use any of the three methods to chunk down your goals. By breaking down your goals and tackling them in bite-sized pieces, you can easily save time and achieve your goals.

5 of the Biggest Productivity Killers and How to Overcome Them

We all aspire to become good time managers and achieve high levels of productivity. However, we experience several obstacles and distractions hinder us from achieving the goals before we can even think of surpassing such goals.

In this section of the chapter, you will discover severe time-wasters and top productivity killers.

1. Busyness
Activities in this category include calling unnecessary meetings, making unnecessary phone calls, organizing email, and cleaning the desk. Most people indulge in excess busywork for the sake of being busy. When you indulge in these non-substantial activities, you are not productive.

How to overcome: set aside one hour per day to delegate all these tasks. Then, you can easily focus on your high priority list of items.

2. Excessive planning
With planning, you are sure you won't miss any important thing. You already know your next actions, and you can focus on your goals with your task list. However, rather than do any actual work, it's much easier to spend time to update and organize your calendar.

How to overcome: set aside one day in 21 days to review undone tasks. Also, spend 15 minutes each morning to review your previous day's performance and update your goals for the day. Evernote and Day One apps are quite useful for this purpose.

3. Less sleep

One of the biggest productivity killers is sleeping less and staying up late. When you sleep less, you do things slowly because it is tough for you to get moving. Hence, you become addicted to coffee before you can have a productive day.

While it may not be necessary to get a full eight hours of sleep, ensure you get enough sleep that makes you productive for the day. Thus, you avoid relying on chemicals which can pose a severe health issue in the nearest future.

4. Email inbox

Email is highly addictive, and it is the biggest time sucker in business or personal life. Worse, you won't get any work done. When you email a client or colleague, and you discuss work, you are not dealing with your problems but helping others solve their problem.

3 simple and effective ways to overcome email overwhelm:

1. Check your email three times per day. This can be an hour before you get to work, after lunch, and just before you sleep. Thus, you can be sure you're not missing out anything.
2. Use Boomerang for Gmail to schedule replies and set up reminders to follow up on sent emails. Thus, you are in control of your time because you can send all your replies at once.
3. Don't write more than a paragraph of response to your email. A better and more effective option is to make a quick call, then, write a short email to act as the paper trail.

When I implemented this technique, I spend less than an hour on emails instead of two hours. I tracked my time using RescueTime,

5. Multitasking

Multitasking means switching between tasks constantly. As humans, our brains can't handle several complex tasks simultaneously. When you multitask, you are unproductive because you produce less quality work, make more mistakes and sometimes, lose more money.

How to overcome: Reread the previous sections in this chapter.

Chapter 5 - Dealing with Distractions

The Difference Between Internal and External Distractions

Before differentiating between internal and external distractions, here's an explanation about each of them.

Internal Distractions
Internal distractions are generated from our self-image and perceptions; they come from our inside. You are experiencing internal distractions each time your plan for a day is delayed or hindered by your thoughts or self-perceptions. Unruly negative ego (especially, lack of self-acceptance, lack of self-love, or both) is usually the primary cause of internal distractions. It involves your desire to be in control to change others or make specific changes about yourself. These thoughts eventually become a self-imposed internal struggle, which leads to frustration.

Compared to internal distractions, it is easier to overcome external distractions. You need to be in control of your mind to overcome internal distractions. That is, you must be mentally disciplined. When you have lots of things on your mind, you will be less productive. For example, you will struggle to focus when you have a health issue, are dehydrated or haven't gotten enough sleep. Also, if you are experiencing some challenges in your relationship, you will struggle to focus.

More importantly, internal distractions prevent you from doing actual work. When you don't have a real purpose or mission, you do nothing. If you don't spend sufficient time to consider your real goals (whether long-term or short-term goals), you won't do anything. You must spend the time to plan your week and days, then, commit to doing what moves you closer to your goals.

Thus, you will avoid sitting in a reactive mode, waiting for someone to provide you with what to come or for the world to work for you. Thus, you can manage your time properly and be truly productive. When you experience internal distractions (which is bound to happen), you must leave them for their proper time. Otherwise, you won't focus on being productive with your time.

External Distractions
There are a lot of external distractions that can affect your focus negatively. You need to pay attention to some of these distractions because they are vital.

Examples;

- Your child needs a ride home because she called in sick from school.
- Your best client needs your attention because he's struggling with a severe challenge

While these external distractions can and does happen, they are not frequent enough to affect your productivity. However, most external distractions shouldn't command your attention because they aren't that important. Examples of unimportant external distractions include countless novelties and trivialities on the internet or conversation about the walking dead, game of thrones or any other popular television shows.

Generally, everything else that you can use as an excuse not to plan or execute your plan is an external distraction.

If you are disciplined and thoughtful enough, you can shut down, turn off, and avoid external distractions.

You will discover proven ways to eliminate external distractions later in this chapter.

Types of Internal Distractions

In this section, you will discover the types of internal distractions that exist. The usual emphasis is on eliminating distractions, but you need to know the types of internal distractions before you can prevent or get rid of them. Knowing the types will help you to realize your kind of inner distraction and the best way to eliminate it.

Type 1: Self-doubt
Insecurity (and not lack of talent) is the biggest killer of dreams. You can turn your self-doubt to a self-fulfilling prophecy when you believe things such as:

"I can't compete with other businesses" or

"I'll never get promoted."

Regardless of your confidence, there are times you are going to experience a little self-doubt. It happens to all of us. However, you must be mentally healthy to prevent self-doubt so that you can achieve your goals.

Self-doubt makes you lose your self-confidence. Self-doubt can make you quit before reaching your goal. This is a significant distraction. Boosting your self-esteem is the best way to get rid of this inner distraction. A few ways you can improve your self-confidence are:

1. *Staying focused on the present*

For example, you are running out into an athletic field or on a stage, but within you, you're thinking, "I will embarrass myself." This thought will affect your performance negatively. Instead of allowing your inner monologue to pull you down, focus on the present. Remind yourself that you don't need to strive for perfection; you only need to do your best. Thus, you can pour in all your energy to achieve better performance.

2. *Control your emotions*

Your thoughts and actions are highly dependent on your emotions. Unless you take proactive measures to control your emotions, anxious feelings can trigger doubtful thoughts and mar your performance.

Monitor the influence of your emotions on your choices. Control your anxiety and calm your mind by distracting yourself with mundane tasks, going for a walk, or taking deep breaths. Don't cave in, give up, or bail out on account of your short-term discomfort.

3. *Ask yourself, "What's the worst thing that can happen?"*

Wild predictions such as "I'm going to mess up everything" can lead to self-doubt. When these doubtful thoughts start creeping in, consider the worst-case scenario. Should you make a mistake, how bad would be the consequences of your error? The truth is, any mistake is not likely to be life-altering. Failing to get a promotion, stumbling over your lines or losing a game won't be that relevant in a few years. So, calm your nerves by keeping things in proper perspective.

4. *Consider the evidence supports your distracting thoughts*

Ask yourself, "What's the proof that I can't or can do this?" Your answer to this question will give you a realistic perspective. Though this technique won't eliminate all your self-doubt, it will reduce it significantly.

5. *Don't worry about a little self-doubt*

According to a 2010 study published in the Psychology of Sport And Exercise, slight insecurity can lead to better performance. When you're aware that things might not go according to plan, create a few minutes to plan how you can improve. This few minutes of planning will help you, in the long run, to utilize your time correctly. Self-confidence remains the best way to eliminate self-distractions.

Type 2: Overthinking and distressful thoughts

If you're fretting about how you will succeed tomorrow or beating up yourself over a mistake you made yesterday. Then, you are suffering from distressful thoughts. Thus, you are in a constant state of anguish, and you are unable to get out of your head.

Though we all over-think things now and then, it shouldn't be too constant. Two of the destructive thought patterns in this internal monologue are worrying and ruminating.

Ruminating involves going over previous actions. Examples of ruminating thoughts include:

- I spoke up too soon at the meeting today. I could tell from their eyes that they thought I was an idiot.
- I was stupid to have left my old job. If I had stayed, I would have been happier.
- My parents were right. I won't amount to anything.

Worrying involves negative predictions about your future. Examples include:

- My presentation tomorrow will be embarrassing. Everyone will conclude that I'm not competent because my hands will be shaking and my face will turn red throughout the presentation.

- It doesn't matter what I do; my promotion will never happen.
- I'm no longer good enough for my spouse. He/she will divorce me and find someone else.
- I should help Edward with his task and destroy my time management plan for the day because Edward helped during my previous task.

Sometimes, distressful thoughts can be in the form of negative imaginations such as imagining your car veering off the road. Overthinking everything prevents you from taking any productive activity.

Effects of overthinking
Overthinking can have a severe negative impact on your well-being.

Evidence from an NCBI research suggests that you are more susceptible to mental health problems when you dwell on your problems, mistakes, or shortcomings. Your tendency to ruminate increases as your mental health declines, leading to a vicious cycle that you may never break.

Another study also showed that severe emotional distress could be the result of overthinking. When you can't sleep even after shutting your mind, then, you know you are an overthinker. With fewer hours of sleep and more reduced sleep quality, your time management for the next day will completely poor because you will desire more rest.

Type 3: Shiny object syndrome
Shiny object syndrome involves distraction through new products, tools, and ideas. These 'bright shiny objects' seem more fun and more exciting than your current projects. Sometimes, you may even think

this new project has more prospects than the project you are working on at the moment.

If you can relate to any of the following, then, you are suffering from shiny object syndrome:

- Rather than complete what you are currently doing, you continuously jump from one goal to another
- You are fascinated by the wild claims of various e-courses. Thus, you jump to another e-course without implementing what you learn from the previous one.
- Instead of executing one of your business ideas, you keep compiling a list of business ideas.
- Rather than build the basics, you spend too much time on new ideas and tools, 95% of which is noise.

One of the best ways to overcome shiny object syndrome is getting into the habit of completing a task before moving to the next one. In the next section of this chapter, you will discover proven ways to silence internal distractions.

13 Ways to Silence Internal Distractions

In the previous section, we discussed the types of internal distractions, but we didn't discuss how to stop them except for the first type of distraction. In this section, you will discover how to silence types two and three internal distractions. Also, you will find other ways to silence internal distractions.

4 Ways to Stop Overthinking
You can limit your negative thinking patterns with consistent practice. Here are the six proven ways to stop overthinking:

Time Management

1. Start paying attention to the way you think
The first step to putting an end to overthinking is awareness. When you observe that you're replaying events in your mind repeatedly, bring yourself to the conscious fact that your thoughts can't change the past.

2. Learn to recognize and replace thinking errors
Since negative thoughts can be highly exaggerated, you must acknowledge and replace them with positive thoughts. Otherwise, you may erroneously assume that you will be fired for calling in sick or that you will become homeless because you forget a deadline.

3. Focus on solving the problem
Looking for solutions is more helpful than dwelling on your problems. Deduce lessons from a mistake or develop steps to prevent a future issue. Always ask yourself, what can I do about it? Rather than asking, why did this happen?

4. Create time to reflect
A little time of reflection can help you to manage your time for the rest of the day properly. Through your meditation, you should identify possible holes in your plan or what you could differently to be successful. Your daily schedule should include 20 minutes of thinking time. Allow your mind to wander excessively during this time. Then, when the 20 minutes is up, move into productive tasks. When you observe that you've started overthinking outside your thinking time, remind yourself that you will think about it later. You may have to repeat this reminder more than once before it becomes effective.

5 Tips to Overcome Shiny Object Syndrome
It is when you are focused that you can manage your time satisfactorily and get things done. But you need to avoid shiny object syndrome

before you can become entirely focused. Here are five proven tips to overcome shiny object syndrome:

1. Learn to differentiate between real opportunities and shiny objects

Shiny objects are actual distractions that disguise as excellent and exciting tools. For example, some new tools are being introduced into the market that makes a lot of bold claims. But won't add value to your productive work or life. Real opportunities must have an actual impact on your life or work. For example, tools that improve your product or service delivery and tools that can boost your workflow.

2. Use the "wait and see" technique

Use this technique when you're unsure about your next decision. Many tools are fast becoming obsolete within a couple of years due to rapid technological advancements. If new software is introduced into the market and claiming to make you more productive, critically analyze whether or not you need that tool. You should only buy this new tool when you are sure that you have no alternative.

3. Remove low-quality information sources

Managing sources of distraction is one of the best ways to manage distraction. When you subscribe to newsletters that recommend new products frequently, you will always struggle to focus because you want to assess each product before making a purchase decision. This is called cognitive load. Your best option is to remove low-quality information sources rather than using your precious mental energy to sieve out the noise. Evaluate your email subscriptions, Facebook group memberships, and social media news feeds. Unsubscribe from groups and newsletters that offer unhelpful, irrelevant suggestions.

4. Don't follow the bandwagon
Assess the suitability of a new tool for your work and life before buying it. Don't buy it or use it because your colleagues are calling it the best thing to happen since sliced bread. This new tool can become your source of unproductivity. Always ask yourself these three critical questions:

- What are the merits vs. demerits of doing this?
- What value will this add to my life or work?
- Do I need it?

If you are genuinely sure that it will add value to your work and life, then, do it.

5. Don't waste your time chasing trends
If you continuously follow every new tool and idea, you won't get things done. You will only be wasting your time chasing trends. Also, understand that a new product doesn't mean it's a better product.

4 Other Ways to Overcome Internal Distractions
Now, here are four other ways to silence any form of internal distractions:

1. Practice cognitive defusion
Most of our intrusive thoughts are rhetorical and abstract. One effective way to lose the power of your negative thoughts is to reframe those thoughts until they lose their meaning. Cognitive defusion is a technique that changes a word or phrase and how it impacts you. For example, if you always repeat a phrase such as "life is meaningless," you can reframe it to "I'm having a thought that life is meaningless." Repeating the reframed sentence removes any negativity out of it. Similarly, if you hear a word in your head repeatedly when you feel

inadequate ('loser') or mess up ('stupid'), saying it out repeatedly dilutes its power. The key is to verbalize the thought so that you can hear it.

A similar technique to cognitive defusion is called the positive effect or positive direction. As the name suggests, this technique involves reframing negative words into positive words. You can turn words such as "I can't do this" into "Of course, I can be successful." "I will never achieve this goal" becomes "I'm definitely going to make this happen." When you use such positive phrasing, you prime your frontal lobes and consequently, stimulate a goal-directed behavior.

2. *Practice self-compassion*
Self-compassion is the act of treating yourself with kindness. You use a gentle understanding and soothing to respond to your anxiety. When you start having anxious thoughts such as "Oh no, here we go. I can't take this. I hate these thoughts."

Self-compassion can turn this internal dialogue to "It's not easy to feel this way, but you can overcome these problems and complete the task." This technique lessens the effects of the anxiety by encouraging you not to blame yourself for feeling anxious. It helps you to approach the fear from a place of understanding.

3. *Verbalize your thoughts*
Since what's floating in your head is often a bunch of unordered thoughts and worries, talking in your head rarely reveals anything significant. However, when you verbalize your feelings and fears, you can develop a story and identify the meaning of the story. If you don't like to a person, journal it. The effects are similar.

Writing helps with physical and psychological issues since it leads to the development of a coherent narrative over time. It is the cognitive processing during writing that makes it a therapeutic activity. By creating a description, you can have an idea of what's happening. Hence, reducing part of those awful cycle of mind chatter.

Another writing technique is to write out the tasks you want to achieve within the next hour. Then, set a deadline for you to finish the tasks. The act of writing out your critical hourly tasks will refocus your brain on your most vital projects. Adding a deadline creates a sense of urgency that helps you to remain focused.

4. *Practice mindfulness and meditation*

If you're stuck in your head and need a quick grounding in the present, mindfulness can be more accessible. It is slightly different from meditation. The best description of mindfulness is by Jon Kabat-Zinn, *"Focus on the present moment on purpose without being judgmental."*

At every moment, always refocus your attention on what you're doing at that moment. Take a moment to focus on the present instead of what's in your head. Thus, you can snap yourself out of your internal distractions when it happens.

6 Reliable Ways to Defeat External Distractions

External distractions usually derails our daily work ethic. This can be anything from your neighbor's little child running past your office window, an unexpected knock on the front door, or a colleague stopping by for a chat. You could be distracted by notifications from Skype, social media newsfeeds, or email.

Most times, we are at fault for these distractions. Most of us are guilty of checking Facebook newsfeeds or email when we should be doing actual work. At other times, distractions happen just like life happens.

Hence, you must regain your concentration instantly to prevent the busyness from consuming your minds.

Since prevention is better than cure, you must find proven ways to minimize these distractions. When our attempts to prevent distractions fail, it's crucial that you have strategies in place to deal with them. Here are six reliable ways of defeating external distractions:

1. Attention firewalling

In recent years, famous figures such as Merlin Mann, Gina Trapani, and Tim Ferriss have made this concept popular in productivity circles. This technique involves preventing distractions rather than dealing with it.

You must track your activities and identify the distractions that prevent you from doing productive work. For instance, you can use software to block access to a specific website that wastes too much of your time. If it remains a distraction because you could bypass the software. You can prevent it by using your router. Since you will need to reset the router and save the change, it would be a bit harder to bypass the router. During that time, you won't be distracted by the internet, and you have a high probability of focusing and refocusing on your tasks when you are distracted.

For email, uninstall notifiers and change the settings of your phone to silent to avoid the beeping sounds of new messages.

2. Keep your to-do list readily visible

Keeping your to-do list nearby makes it easier to get back on task during your waiting period and keep your focus clear. Hence, you can avoid falling into the distraction trap. Also, ensure you write your to-do list legible such that you can read it from your most common working position.

Set up little reminder messages such as "are you on task?" to help you regain focus during times you start wandering. The real secret is to make your task list visible all the time and be mindful of it.

3. Keep a procrastination pad.

This procrastination pad can be by your desk or on your computer. Jot notes about your distractions in them as they come. Thus, you can forget about them and come back to them later. An alternative is to use a separate device to store your distractions. For example, you can have a jotter titled "procrastination pad," which contains your distractions.

4. Maximize your productivity peaks

We all have specific periods of the day where we are at peak productivity. You need to identify these times and give yourself the best advantage by scheduling your most important for these times.

5. Psyche yourself up to work

A compelling reason to complete work is highly essential in staying on task. Remind yourself about the benefits of finishing your task. For example, a work-free weekend or the pride in finishing a challenging project. Reminding yourself of some short-term benefits also works. For example, if you complete a specific amount of work, you can have enough time to rest and take your wife on a date for the night.

6. Use the instant-reward technique

Tell yourself you would do something entertaining for 10 minutes once you can complete your next task within a specific timeframe. For example, if you complete 600 words of an article within the next 30 minutes, you will play your favorite game on your phone for 5 minutes. If your work allows you to work remotely, you can use this technique to sharpen your focus. However, this method should be your last resort because it's almost impossible to do your best work within

20- or 30-minute timeframes. It's a good strategy when you are too distracted or when you struggle to start your day with productive work.

Chapter 6 - Emulating Success

Goal Setting Examples from The Business Masters

In this section, we explore the goal-setting secrets of some great business executives. Let's get started:

1. Barbara Corcoran

Barbara is a "Shark Tank" investor and founder of Barbara Corcoran Inc.

"Due to time constraints, I usually organize my list in sections. The first section is for calls I intend to make, but it doesn't exceed three calls. I put my calls into the first section to avoid forgetting about them.

The review section is my second section. These are typically short tasks. In it, I answer questions such as 'Would you like to be on our show?' I can do a quick review and get it out of the way since the relevant paperwork is attached to it. Though they are not listed in any particular order, I ensure I complete them in less than a day.

The third section is my project list. These contain tasks that move my business forward and make me money. I further categorize them as A, B, and C, depending on importance. Some of the tasks in this list are companies I've invested in through Shark Tank. *The A tasks are essential and today-only. The B tasks are also necessary, but their deadline is not today.*

When my task list is too small, it shows that I haven't created time for reflection. My list grows more substantial when I have more time to reflect. When I reflect, I'm able to think of new opportunities that I don't want to forget. Despite trying various to-do lists, my useful to-do lists have been the ones typed or written. There is a satisfaction that I get with crossing off tasks that I can't get with using the delete button."

2. Jim McCann

Jim is the author of *Talk is (Not) Cheap: The Art of Conversation Leadership* and the founder and CEO of 1-800-flowers.com, Inc.

"I've been using lists for most parts of my business life. I had a crazy list-maker as a mentor at St. John's home in Queens, New York. Being busy is easy, but being effective is a lot harder. Using my mentor's example, I bought a pad and printed 'things I have to do today' on it. Currently, I combine physical and digital pads. My list is divided into four:

- Things I must do today
- A general to-do list
- A projects list
- A long-term ideas list. These are highly important for the company's growth.

Before assigning my jottings to any of the lists above, I ask myself one question: 'Must it be done today?' Most of these jottings are useful ideas that fit for the long-term ideas list or the projects list. My team assesses these lists from time to time to determine whether or not the ideas are still good enough for implementation. We replace the ideas that are no longer good enough with new ones. With a proper task list, you can become a better manager of your time."

3. Jim Koch

Jim Koch is the founder of the Boston Beer Company.

"Priority tasks from different internal teams determine my day. Every morning, I write down a maximum of five must-do goals for that day on a Post-it note. This act keeps me focused for the day.

While these items not necessarily urgent, they are important. Once I start my day, I ensure that the list remains reachable to avoid procrastinating on them. However, I strike out all items on the list by the close of each day. Also, each of my weeks starts with a maximum of five emails in my inbox. To ensure that issues or questions are resolved pretty quickly, I respond to emails almost immediately after I receive them. Thus, responding to emails doesn't affect my productivity during my daily breaks.

During my break-time, I switch off my internet and spend that time at the nearest hardware store. I may even pick up a tool I need at home. By the time I return to my desk, I will make headway with my previous issue or dilemma."

4. Daymond John

Daymond is the founder of the famous clothing line, FUBU, and he is the author of the *Power of Broke*.

"I have a set of 10 goals. The first seven goals are 6-month goals. The rest are 5-year, 10-year, and 20-year goals. Since I want my goals to be the last thing I think and dream about, I make it a habit to read my goals every morning and every night. I write down the seven goals on a piece of paper. While each goal has an expiry date, I include a few details of how I will achieve each goal. The first five goals are health, family, business, relationship, and philanthropy goals. The next two are personal financial goals and business project goals. Each goal is written in a positive language. For example, if my goal is to reduce my weight to 170 pounds by July 5. The few details would be to eat fish, drink eight glasses of water daily, and exercise twice per day. It won't include avoiding alcohol, meat, and fried foods."

5. Yunha Kim

Yunha is the founder and CEO of Simple Habit, a meditation app.

"Setting time limits is one of my workflow secrets. We often have never-ending lists of to-dos at a startup like ours. Hence, it is not feasible to fully finish a task in one sitting."

13 Time Management Hacks of Successful People

It is not easy to manage or maximize your time. But by knowing the tips and tricks of today's most successful people, you can use their tips or develop your time management strategies. Thus, improving your productivity. Learn more about various unconventional time-saving tricks from the time management tricks of some of the world's most successful people.

1. Sir Richard Branson delegates emails
Sir Richard is the founder of the Virgin group. He is also a British business magnate, investor, author, and philanthropist.

"I check reader emails in the morning. I pass some to colleagues, dictate the ones with quick answers to my assistants. But I write the more detailed responses personally. I check my email in bursts to focus on my current tasks. I give my employees space rather than directives. I am comfortable allowing them to take responsibility because I hired people I trust."

2. Jack Dorsey creates daily themes
Jack is the CEO and co-founder of payment processing experts, Square and social media company, Twitter. Dorsey runs these two significant companies simultaneously by giving each day a theme. Dorsey spends each day of the week to focus on a particular primary area. For example, Mondays can be for product development, and Tuesdays can be for general management functions. Wednesdays can be buffer days where you respond to low-priority emails and tasks.

Time Management

3. Mary Callahan Erdoes uses the calendar for day-to-day management

"The biggest tool to manage time is calendar management. Focus on controlling your calendar. Create a list of you expect from others and what others expect from you. If you don't control your calendar, it will end up controlling you."

4. Barack Obama limits his outfits

Barack Obama is the former president of the united states.

"I pare down decisions by wearing only blue or gray suits. Since I have too many decisions to make, I prefer to exclude eating and wearing decisions out of it by paring down my decisions."

5. Jack Groetzinger tracks his time

Jack is the co-founder and CEO of SeatGeek.

"I have an estimated period for each of my tasks. I have software that records when I start and finish each item on my task list. I push myself to accomplish an efficiency goal for each day. My efficiency goal is actual minutes divided by expected minutes. I have fun gamifying my to-do list because I own all the spots on the leaderboard."

6. Gary Vaynerchuk uses other people's time

Gary Vaynerchuk is a business coach and the CEO of VaynerchukMedia.

"I scale my time efficiency using other people. I can focus on my personal and professional priorities by having others do the tasks that must be done. One of my assistants works full-time as my health coach. He oversees my exercise and nutrition. The other assistant follows me around and films me. As my time becomes more valuable, I may hire a full-time driver rather than waiting for a ride."

Pro Tip: If you can't afford to hire full-time assistants, you can hire virtual assistants or outsource some of your tasks to them.

7. Steve Ballmer creates a time budget

Steve is the ex-CEO of Microsoft. Steve has a spreadsheet accessible by his assistants where he budgets time to those who need to speak with him or meet him. Thus, he manages his time by spending most of his time on important things.

8. Adora Cheung is strict about meetings

Adora Cheung is the CEO of Homejoy, an online platform that connects customers with home service providers. Adora sends a Google Doc to potential meeting participants. These participants write down the agenda for the meeting. After prioritizing the topics, Adora does not discuss any plan that's not on the list.

9. Tony Hsieh uses Yesterbox

Tony Hsieh is the CEO of the famous shoe and clothing line, Zappos. Tony recommends responding to yesterday's emails today. Hence, today's emails won't clutter your focus for the day. He terms this technique as "Yesterbox." One capable app that can help you to achieve inbox zero is called boomerang. It helps you to give proper attention to specific emails by resending those emails into your inbox as new emails at your specified time.

10. Arianna Huffington eats meals away from her desk

Arianna Huffington is the author of 15 books, the founder of the *Huffington Post* and the founder/CEO of Thrive Global. She recommends *not* working while taking meal breaks during the day. *"Take a colleague and have lunch at a table far away from your desk or go to a cafeteria. This shouldn't take more than 20 minutes. Doing this is more recharging than eating lunch while working, which is what* many of us do. It can be the difference between having a productive or an unproductive end to your day."

11. Mark Cuban uses email for most interactions

Mark Cuban is an American investor and businessman. He co-owns 2929 Entertainment, owns the Dallas Mavericks (an American basketball team), and is an investor in "Shark Tank." Rather than waste time in long meetings or on lengthy phone calls, Mark Cuban uses email for most conversations and become more productive. *"Email saves me hours every day. No phone calls, no meetings, and I set my schedule. Unless I'm picking up a check, all other things are email. I love it, and I live on it."*

12. Jeff Bezos uses the "Two Pizza Rule"

Jeff is the founder, CEO, and president of Amazon.com. He is also an investor and charity donor. Rather than waste his time in meetings, Bezos maximizes his time by not attending big meetings. To him, a meeting is big if two pizzas can't feed the participants at the meetings.

13. Nick Huzar capitalizes on Sundays

Nick is the CEO and co-founder of OfferUp, which connects local buyers and sellers. *"Plan your work and stick to the plan. I ensure that I create a quiet period for myself on Sundays. During this period, I examine each department at OfferUp to determine the team's priorities. Then, during the week, I support each team to implement these priorities. Also, I'm a sucker for routines. With routines, I'm able to eliminate excuses. For example, the first thing I always do each night is to pack for the next day's gym."*

10 Morning Routines of Groundbreaking Entrepreneurs

Starting your day right is the key to uber-productive days. Your actions at the start of the day will determine whether you will achieve extraordinary or mediocre results. Here's how ten highly successful entrepreneurs maximize their days right from the time they get out of bed.

1. Create a to-do list the previous night

"On alternating days, I work out for an hour and jog to the office. While at the office, I review my to-do list from the previous night. Thus, I can identify my most important tasks and finish them before anything else." - Barbara Corcoran, founder of the Corcoran Group.

2. Start your day with maximum energy

"By waking up early and playing basketball, my starts with the right energy and clarity. After showering, I eat a 3-egg breakfast, which fills me to satisfaction and sharpens my focus. Then, I proceed to achieve a zero-inbox. I help my team with any challenges they're facing. Thus, I have an idea of my challenges for the day. I ponder on my tasks' list for the day and face them squarely." - Tim Draper, founding partner of DFJ - a legendary VC firm.

3. Choose a routine that fits your personality type

"Your personality type can be emotional, social, action, or practical. If you are the emotional type, you are sensitive and might be introverted. Hence, your routine will involve lots of quiet time and introspection. If you are the social type, your daily routine will be people-based. For example, you will love working out in the gym in the presence of at least five people. If you are the action-type personality, you will love a morning routine of variety. You will love to start your day with a combination of jogging, jujitsu, or reading various books, especially books outside your industry. Practical-type

people love a well-structured daily routine. The most important aspect of any routine is sticking with your plan. We all tend to have a morning routine until life happens. So, use your personality type to determine your most effective morning routine." - Tai Lopez, investor and advisor to many multimillion-dollar businesses with an eight-figure online empire.

4. Tune up your brain

"Since I know my day will be busy and probably, unpredictable, I start my day by going for a cold swim in the pool. Then, over a cup of coffee, I play the crossword puzzle in the Los Angeles Times; this rarely exceeds 20 minutes. Then, I get into my office to start working." - Mark Sisson. Mark Sisson is the publisher of marksdailyapple.com (a paleo blog), the best-selling author of the New Primal Blueprint and the founder of the Primal Blueprint.

5. Use nutrition to fire up your brain

"I drink one ounce of water which contains a cleansing mineral. I flush out my system by drinking a quart of structured purified water. Then, I wake up every muscle with a 45-pound kettlebell and 20 minutes of Turkish getups. I provide my brain with the ultimate brain nutrient by taking three milliliters of oceans alive marine phytoplankton. After my shower, I use 30 sprays of ease magnesium for my abdomen before taking a supplement to repair my cells. I eat two farm-fertilized organic chicken eggs and three different types of fruit for my breakfast. Lastly, I take a cup of green smoothie." - Ian Clark. Ian is the founder and CEO of Activation Products.

6. Jumpstart your metabolism

"After getting out of bed by 5:30 am, I drink 20 ounces of water to set my metabolism into action. I write my gratitude list for the morning. Then, I determine my two main priorities for the day. These priorities must move me in the direction of my goals before I can call my day awesome." - Jon Braddock, founder, and CEO of My Life & Wishes.

7. Verbalize your day's intention

"I spend a few minutes to show gratitude for health and body before I get out of bed. Then, I speak out my intention for the day. While setting the intentions for my goals, I drink a glass of water, light some candles, and daydream. I check my emails for important messages before swinging into full work mode." - Elle Russ, Coach and Best-Selling Author of the Paleo Thyroid Solution.

8. Start early

"I get up at 4:15 am and spend 15 minutes of gratitude. By 5 am, I am at the gym to have a bodybuilding session with a personal trainer until 6 am. Between 6:30 and 7 am, I meditate and envision how to achieve my goals and dreams. I spend 30 minutes (7:15 am to 7:45 am) with my family before starting work by 8 am." - Adele McLay, Author, Speaker, and Business Growth Consultant.

9. Start with meditation

"After meditation, I use my five-minute journal before exercising and drinking a protein shake. Then, I help others in my way. Either by making an important introduction, sending a written note of gratitude or posting a #ploughshare online. I spend some time to write or draw images. Lastly, I take one major step to achieve my goal." - Chris Plough, Serial Entrepreneur and Entrepreneur Advisor.

10. Block off times of solitude

"Being a father of young children, an entrepreneur, and a doctor, my days can become highly disorder without proper planning. After getting up by 6:30 am, I spend a minimum of 30 minutes in complete and peaceful solitude before having a cup of coffee. To get into the right state of mind, I pray, read some educational materials, review *my goals for that day, and practice mindful meditation. I strongly engage in a positive-thinking mental state to foster immense power into my mind. When I am not on intermittent fasting, my breakfast is usually light and consists of a few nutritional supplements depending on my current blood test results. Then, I maximize the day by working with full zeal and energy."* - Dr. Nick Zurowski, founder of NuVision Health Center.

I encourage you to use any of these morning routines as they are or more importantly, modify them to suit your lifestyle so that you can enjoy more productive and creative mornings.

Chapter 7 - Regaining Control of The Future

15 Effective Time Management Habits

If you have read this far, you would have identified some time management habits already. Some were discussed in the previous chapter as examples from business masters, successful people, and groundbreaking entrepreneurs. Others have been discussed in previous chapters. Hence, they won't be repeated in this chapter. Instead, you will discover more proven time management tips that you can incorporate into your daily life.

1. Learn to speed-read

While you cannot avoid all the barrage of information being thrown at you, you can sort them and go through them at your pace and time. Learning to speed-read is one of the most important skills you can develop. Have you ever taken a course in speed reading? If no, enroll for one now. With new technologies now available, you can read up to 1,000 words per minute and comprehend most of what you have read.

2. Stack your reading

Print and file important pieces of information, summaries, or valuable items. Alternatively, you can collate them in a separate file on your computer and read them later. Rather than lose focus on your current task, you can file away that piece of information and read them later. Once this becomes a habit, you will be amazed at how much you can give to what you read and how much more you read. Whether you are reading the paper version or electronic version of your newspapers, skim and read what's relevant to you. When you are reading the news, bear in mind that most of the information is always in the headline and first paragraph. Most times, you rarely need to read the remaining details to understand the story fully.

3. Only read what is important and relevant

The design of all magazines and newspapers is to make you read each page of the magazine or newspaper. The reason is for you to view all the advertisements in magazines or newspapers. Thus, you must read what matters to you only. After reviewing the table of contents, head to the information that is relevant to your life and work. The "rip and read" technique is an exceptional technique for printed materials. Rip out and file articles you intend to read. Then, carry the file with you to read during your timeouts. Similarly, read book reviews before spending time to read the complete book. You can get the main gist of the book by reading the book's review. Instead of scouring the web to read reviews, it is more convenient to subscribe to book review services.

4. Organize your work environment

For many people, they believe that a messy work environment and a cluttered desk aids their work efficiency. However, various research has shown that when people work in a clean, ordered environment and focus only on one task, their productivity almost triples instantly. People with a cluttered work environment spend copious time seeking the materials they need to work effectively. Psychologically, a cluttered work environment affirms your belief that you lack organization. Hence, you are continuously distracted by all the items you are seeing.

5. Maximize your mornings

Set your alarm clock for a couple of hours earlier than normal when you have deadlines to hit and projects to complete. I've found this to be more effective than trying to work extra in the evening when you're too tired to focus. You can get some dedicated time by going to bed an hour earlier than your usual time. In the early morning hours, your mind is alert, you're refreshed, the house is quiet, and you are at peak productivity. Spend this extra hour on one item of your task list. A half-hour earlier in the day is an additional 23 days over the year. This is as good as buying time. Imagine that!

6. Map out your weekly meals

Consider your schedules, special occasions, and items on the grocery list to plan your meal for the week. Remember to review the pantry to ensure that all the ingredients for items on your grocery list are completely available. Also, go to the supermarket with a proper plan, there should be no impulse purchase. When you make it a habit to plan your meal once a week, you won't waste time pondering on what to eat. A side benefit is that you eat healthier.

You can apply the weekly meal plan to other aspects of your life. For example, choose a day to plan the clothes you will wear for the week. Then, ensure you wash them and make them ready for your use.

7. Be in the present

Abandon all your baggage from the previous day in the past. Don't allow your previous day's failures, embarrassments, losses, disappointments, and mistakes to affect the joy you will likely experience today. Start your day by expecting to experience a day of relationship building, fulfillment, and success. Maximize your time to enjoy the best return on each day of your life.

8. Establish rules for your time

Establish rules for your time when creating your schedule. Turn off your cell phone during your timeout, for example, during breakfast. Set aside blocks of time that you will not be available to people and devices.

9. Audit your time

Assess your current time spending habits for the next seven days. Record your activities in a journal or on your phone. Split your activities into one-hour blocks. Then, answer the following questions:

- What did you accomplish?
- Was it a complete waste of time?
- Did you spend the time to your satisfaction?

Use the priority matrix discussed in chapter four to log your activities in the appropriate quadrant. Add the numbers after seven days. So, which quadrant did you spend the most time? Don't be surprised by your answer.

10. Eliminate your bad habits

Bad habits are one of our biggest time wasters. Those bad habits eliminate our precious little time. Hence, if you are serious about achieving big goals in your life, and spend your time wisely, ensure you eliminate those bad habits. Examples of time-wasting habits include going out to drink with friends frequently, playing games, excessively surfing social media, and Netflix binge-watching.

11. Find a mentor

When you don't have someone to guide you, you can quickly get distracted and dissuaded. But it's easier to stay on track with your time when you can personally rely on someone who's been through the same process. Thus, he can help you achieve your goals faster.

12. Don't wait for inspiration

You are wasting time by waiting to start a project. Since there is no perfect time to do anything, throw away the excuses that are preventing you from getting started. While I'm not suggesting that you should be impatient, you should identify what you intend to accomplish and take immediate action towards it.

13. Engage in hobbies

Hobbies engage in parts of your brain that you don't use for work. Thus, you become more creative and can solve problems with ease. You can achieve success by spending some time outside of your comfort zone. If you're a software developer, go out and socialize. If you're pianist, practice martial arts. If you're a lawyer, learn to dance.

14. Have a great time

Don't become obsessed about marking off all the tasks on your task list. Balance your work and life to enjoy your day. It's not worth it to complete an oversized workload one day only to have an unproductive, burnt-out day the next day. Work at your best pace. When you rush through tasks, you become stressed and produce substandard work.

15. Meditate

A few minutes of meditation can improve your focus and calmness. Thus, your work becomes more efficient, and your contribution is more significant. Also, meditation brings your mind back to the present to help you avoid several distractions. When your mind is in the present, you can accomplish a lot more within a small time-span. Meditation improves your awareness. Thus, we rarely make mistakes at work, and you save the time you're supposed to use to correct your errors. Meditation can also strengthen your intuition. A strong intuition enhances your decision-making ability and consequently, saves you time.

Defeating Perfectionism Once and for All

Though our current world expects us to be perfect in always, it doesn't mean that perfectionism is the way to a successful life. Like an obsessive-compulsive disorder, your desire for perfection can mess you up. And since it makes you lose perspective as you get deeper into it, it messes up those around you. Since none of us can become perfect, you will only be driving yourself crazy, trying to achieve an elusive goal. Perfectionism can lead to depression. Research by Sydney Blatt, a psychologist at Yale University showed that perfectionists are more likely to kill themselves than regular people.

To avoid the perfectionist trap, implement these seven proven steps:

1. Practice failing

Doing exercises where you will likely fail is one of the most effective ways to defeat perfectionism. So, learn a new skill that requires a lot of falling and embarrassment. It will teach you that tolerance of failure, self-compassion, and patience are part of the learning curve.

For example, I joined a racing group of paddlers despite having been on a paddleboard only a couple of times. This group consists of people who paddle at least 21 miles in the ocean and perform those cool 360 turns on their boards. I spent most of the evening in the water and not on it, but I am now more comfortable with failing. I realize that the world won't end because I am the worst person in a group of athletes. I will do my best to translate this lesson into other areas of my life, where I am anxious or depressed due to perfectionism.

2. Differentiate between goals and dreams

Since it is highly probable that they won't happen, grand ideas usually create lots of angst. For example, one of my friends used to dream of playing professional basketball. Nothing wrong in having a dream, right? But he started having behavioral issues because he was placed in the C team of his basketball team. When he's on his good behavior, he will practice his shots and improve his techniques for hours daily. But he always plays badly during games because he was exerting too much pressure on himself. When I feel like my expectations were weighing too much on me, I usually write down my goals on a piece of paper. Then, I will check off the realistic ones. But I will tweak the silly ones to avoid putting myself under undue pressure.

3. Be a hard worker

It is often said that smart people cut corners. However, knowing which corners to cut is the art of being a star performer. Hence, the way out is to analyze your goal in all honesty critically. Then, identify any perfectionism in the plan for each purpose. Most times, we hide under perfectionism to avoid taking actions to accomplish our real goals. The truth is, a proper plan, hard work, and a bit of luck are required to achieve any real intent. But most perfectionists don't agree that luck is involved in achieving any goal.

4. Keep yourself in check

Keep yourself in check when your self-doubt is becoming more real, or you start having reasons to believe your inner critic. Use these questions to give yourself a reality check:

- Are my thoughts based on facts, or are they the figment of my imagination?
- Why am I making unfavorable verdicts?
- Is the situation as bad as I imagine it?
- What's the worst thing that can happen? Is it likely to happen?
- Will this be important in the next five years? Will this be an issue at vital moments of my life? Examples of essential moments include childbirth, moving to another city, or moving abroad.

By the time I complete answering these questions, I often realize that I was only trying to validate various falsehoods in my head. Sometimes, I even forgot how I got into this frightening state in the first place. Apart from giving reassuring our self-esteem, this reality test also makes less dependent on others for affirmative compliments.

5. Be kind to yourself

As a perfectionist, you often criticize others. It is a proven fact that this criticism is a defense mechanism. It causes you to pick on the shortcomings in others rather than accept those shortcomings in yourself or accept that no human being is perfect. The more you identify your weaknesses, the more you look out for it in those around you. You do this because you have created an ideal image of the perfect person and life, but you can't seem to separate this idealized version from reality. A simple and effective way to reduce this habit significantly is to be kind to yourself. When you like your "flawed and imperfect" self, you're much less likely to be the irritable person who critically analyzes others.

So, try saying one thing you love about yourself each morning. It can be something about your face or a poem about yourself. Anytime you feel you need a boost during the day, repeat this affirmation. Note that nothing stops you from using the same declaration every day or having seven daily affirmations. Thus, you only repeat one affirmation every seven days. Rather than living an unforgiving, locked-down, and hard-hearted life, start being kind to yourself.

6. Refuse fear

Are you afraid of:

- Choosing a partner,
- Making the wrong life decision or
- Starting a new project?

If yes, then, you are exhibiting some of a perfectionist's trait. All the factors above have a common theme: a fear of failure. Thus, we rely on others to guide us and make our decisions for us. But refusing to allow fear to dictate your moves or choice is one of the best ways to combat such behavior.

One way to develop the habit of preventing fear to lead is to automate the start of the sequence. For example, a basketball player is ready to rise and shoot just as he has done a hundred times a day during practice by coming to the free-throw line, touching his socks, shorts, receiving the ball and bouncing it exactly three times.

Similarly, a pro golfer may be chatting with the scorekeeper, a friendly official, his playing partner or his caddie while walking along the fairway. But the moment he stands behind the ball and takes a deep breath, he's telling himself just one thing: focus.

In each of these examples, the athletes were able to replace doubt and fear with comfort and routine. They could do this because they've learned how to automate the start of their sequence. Rather than pretend not to be in the mood because I am afraid to start, I start with the smallest step towards the goal.

7. Be proud of your accomplishments

When we were young, we sketched what we intend to become in the future. However,, most of us never become what we've sketched out. Rather than being an astronaut or petrochemical engineer, you are probably a barista who barely spends time with his loved ones because you work for long periods. As a perfectionist, you need to accept that fact. Stop comparing yourself with others thinking you haven't achieved enough or you may never achieve anything. Instead, be comfortable in your skin and be proud of your accomplishments.

Create a list of your accomplishments in the past week, month, or year. Even the simple things count. The book you finished, that small project you completed with your team or maintaining a clean home. These are your accomplishments without being the neuro-surgeon you imagined when you were five years old.

Like any change, trust and self-examination are some of the requirements to tame any perfectionist tendencies. But if you meet challenges on the way and it seems you aren't moving forward, don't beat yourself up or take yourself too seriously. Find the means to succeed and enjoy the process. Keep in mind that you are solely responsible for your success or failure. So, don't give up.

Tools and Techniques to Take Back Time for Good

Ever heard any or all of these phrases before:
- The emails flooding my inbox is making me lose focus.
- Let me check my social media feed. It won't take 5 minutes!

If you have heard any of these phrases, then, you know the person lacks proper time management. Time management involves organizing tasks and allocating time to specific activities (professional or personal).

Before delving into those tools and techniques, remember that tasks, time, people, and information are the four key areas to any successful time management system. Hence, you should have any of these four essential tools:

- **Notebook**

A good notebook is the most frequently missing too in people's time management systems. Yes, it is good to have a bunch of post-its or a pad of paper on your desk. But you should keep all your notes in one place. Thus, when you need to retrieve any piece of information, you can go to this place.

- **Address Book**

Most people do not see the value of a good address book because we now live in a uber-connected world. However, when you need to connect with valuable contact, LinkedIn, Instagram, Facebook, or Twitter may disappoint you. Your best option is to save all contact's phone numbers and email addresses in a safe place and treat them like gold.

- **Calendar**

If you don't know how and where you spend your time, it would be difficult to manage it. It is easier for you to schedule, plan, and track your time with a good calendar. You cannot only track the time for your meetings, but you can also track the time for your tasks and projects.

- **To-do list**

A good to-do list is a cornerstone of any productivity system. This one-time management tool should complete your arsenal of tools. However, don't forget to reread the common reasons why to-do lists fail in Chapter 3 of this book.

Thus, you can avoid making those mistakes with your to-do list. Lastly, your to-do list should be with you all the time. Double-check your time management toolkit to ensure that you have all these four essential time management tools.

When you can plan and accomplish your daily routines within specified time frames, then, you are a good manager of time. Thus, you can carry out your activities with more significant commitment.

Fortunately, technology has made it possible to optimize every minute of the day. In this section, you will discover seven tools and techniques that I use, and I am convinced will improve your time management skills and productivity.

1. A time management system

A proper organization of your daily tasks is one of the steps you can take to improve your productivity and not suck at time management. In any self-organization process, creating to-do lists is an essential step. You might have to try a few to-do list methods to discover the one that's most suitable for you. Your to-do list could be a fancy electronic version on your mobile device or computer. But it could be done using old-fashioned pen and paper which you check off after completing each task.

An overview of each significant activity is your first step when you have high-level projects. Then, you can split them into specific tasks and arrange them in the order in which they have to be performed. Don't forget to add deadlines to each task.

Here are three examples of such systems that you can use

- **The Now Habit by Neil Fiore.** This system teaches you to use a reverse order to build your to-do list. Fill your calendar with realistic leisure time, committed activities, and scheduled chores. Then, use different lifestyle and scheduling rules to assign your tasks into the remaining times.
- **The Final Version by Mark Forster.** From the task list, you have written for the day, go through it, and identify the most crucial task. Complete that task, then, identify the next most important task. Complete it and repeat the process till you complete all the task for that day.

- **Getting Things Done by David Allen.** Perform a brain dump of your tasks on paper. Then, rearrange them in order of importance. Next, set a deadline for completion and get to work. Review your execution plans periodically and where necessary, make adjustments.

2. **Wunderlist**

With Wunderlist, you can create task lists, organize them into folders, and set up reminders to alert you when the deadline is close. Wunderlist has an enchanting user interface, and all its features work effectively on all devices (cell phone, tablet, or computer).

3. **Remember The Milk**

The free plan allows you to create tasks and synchronize them on any platform, including your emails. Thus, you can access your tasks anytime. Perfect for managing personal tasks, Remember The Milk is available for Android and iOS.

4. **RescueTime**

Do you always feel that time passes very quickly, and it's almost impossible for you to complete your daily activities? Then, the RescueTime app is your best option. With it, you can track your tasks online. It gauges your progress and reveals the time you spend procrastinating.

5. Todoist or Trello

Todoist is both a cloud-based app and a mobile app. You can access your Todoist tasks on multiple operating systems and even share your tasks with other colleagues. Also, it displays delivery times. You can easily play around with the features because it has an intuitive layout. First, type in your project, then, split them into specific tasks and attach a deadline to each of them. Now, assign a level of priority to each task (there are four priority levels there). You can move the tasks around to suit your available time.

If you have a small team, you can use Trello to visualize your team's projects. Within Trello, you can assign tasks to each team member, set up boards that represent projects and set up various lists within each board. There are a series of cards for each list. The cards represent tasks. For example, you can create a board for a specific project, split the board into lists (the stages of the project), then, arrange each individual's tasks on a series of cards.

6. Relaxation breaks

You must take time out of your work; it will increase your productivity. After a period of sustained concentration, your body needs a release, and your mind needs a timeout. Sometimes, you develop fresh ideas from your timeout. The best way to help this process is to take a 5-minute walk away from your workspace. If you don't take breaks intentionally, your mind will do so for you by wandering when you are tired.

Use the FocusMe app to set enforced breaks or break reminders.

7. Process management technique

When you have personal tasks or business tasks, then, the time management tools and techniques discussed above are excellent. However, when your business grows, and you need to manage bulk processes or team time, then, the process management technique is a more effective system. This technique maps out the primary operations of a company and set deadlines for each task. Also, it adds an alert configuration to serve as the basis of prioritization. Here's how the alert configuration works for an airfare booking task:

- The person in charge receives an email when you reach 50% of the task deadline
- You will see a red visual indicator when you reach 70% of the task deadline
- At 80% of the task deadline, the person in charge receives a new message.

8. Evernote

This free productivity tool allows you to organize your images, thoughts, and ideas in various formats (audio, text, or pictures). Also, you can record your speeches, interviews, and meetings. You can even share your voice or text attachments with your friends. Optimize your time by syncing the Remember The Milk app with Evernote. Arguably, one of Evernote's most useful and popular features is its web clipper. This is similar to bookmarks in web browsers. Web clipper allows you to "clip" paragraphs of text, images or entire webpages to Evernote. Clipped items can be organized, stored, and searched like regular notes. You can even add annotations to "clipped" items in Evernote. You can integrate Evernote with Gmail, Outlook, Google Drive, Microsoft teams, Salesforce, Slack, and most other apps on your mobile devices or PC.

9. MyLifeOrganized (MLO)

If you struggle to organize your goals, work with your to-do lists, or manage all your tasks, this app is your best option. This productivity tool helps you to focus on the actual steps to accomplish your goals. It considers your set priorities (urgency, importance, start date, and terms of completion) to identify your first task automatically.

Conclusion

You can become a master time manager when you practice the techniques and use the tools recommended in this book. Reclaim your time from busywork, have more hours to spend with your loved ones and improve your personal life. The main reason for having improved time management skills is to increase our experience of pleasure, happiness, and the overall quality of our lives. Three things largely determine the quality of your life:

- Inner life
- Health
- Relationships

- **Inner life** involves feeling good about your personality and character, liking yourself and getting along with yourself. It takes time and reflection to improve your inner life.
- **Health.** No level of success is worth having poor health. Most times, the best use of your time involves going to bed early and having a good night's sleep. Also, take time out to get proper rest, exercise regularly, and eat the right foods.
- **Relationships.** Make out time for your loved ones. The most influential people in your life are those you care about and those who care about you. So, don't get caught up in so much at the expense of vital relationships with your loved ones. A balanced life is a great life. You will find greater fulfillment, satisfaction, and joy by enhancing the quality of your life. Let me leave you with the words of a wise old doctor. "Having spoken to lots of people when they are about to die, no

businesses man on his deathbed ever wished to spend more time in his office."

You just learned proven steps and strategies for managing your time efficiently and effectively. That means you can now improve your productivity and achieve your goals. Still, packing away all this information in your head won't do you any good if you don't put it to use. Hence, I encourage you to return to chapter 1 and identify the reasons why you're failing at time management. Then, review the steps in subsequent chapters and start implementing them right away.

When you implement the steps and strategies in this book, you will see a marked improvement in your life. You feel more in control and have more time for yourself. Start every day with an accomplishment that gives you energy. This can be a physical workout or meditation.

At first, implementing these techniques can make you feel uncomfortable. But the rewards can make your day highly productive. You will experience greater confidence because you are more energetic. Once your weekly plans and activities become a habit, challenge yourself to create a monthly plan.

Over time, you should develop a 3-month, 6-month, and an annual plan. Take a weekend off at the end of the year to reflect on the previous year and plan for the new one. Ensure you schedule your events, vacations, and projects into your yearly plan. Planning your future with a well-designed plan can calm your nerves in this world of uncertainty.

When you are in charge of your time, you have improved confidence that's noticeable to others. Saving time involves investing some time to plan, make changes, and improve your life. The most significant single piece of advice I can give you at this point is: do not get lost in the weeds! By this, I mean, do not get lost in every tiny detail.

Getting good at managing your time requires you to take action rather than trying to get every last detail in order. Even if you are feeling unsure about whether or not you're doing things correctly, it is far more important to get started. I can't stress this enough. I promise that results will come with just some practice and some experience. That is the only thing separating you from achieving the goals you desire. Don't worry about whether or not everything is 100% perfect or feeling skeptical whether or not this will work for you. Just do it. All of these excuses will only stunt your growth. Take action now — not tomorrow. Your success depends on the action you take today.

I'm going to challenge you to be accountable. Call a trusted friend and share your goal of better time management. That's right; you're going to be held accountable. Because this time you won't fail. This time you're going to get better at managing your time finally. No matter who you are, you can manage your time with greater efficiency. You deserve this. So, go ahead and get started now, because higher productivity and a better life is waiting for you!

Procrastination Stops Today

Do You Have Countless Ideas and Unfinished Projects? Discover the Simple Way to Shift Your Mindset and Increase Your Productivity by 10X, Even If you're Lazy AF

Table of Contents

Introduction **121**
Chapter One: Beating Laziness **125**
   7 Tactics To Beat Laziness 126
   10 Essential Energy-Boosting Foods 129
   5 Tricks To Get Energized And Stay Energized 133
Chapter Two: Powering Up Productivity **135**
   Getting Things Done (GTD) 135
   Zen To Done Method (ZTD) 137
   8 Productivity Apps You Need In Your Life Right Now 139
   12 Morning Routine Habits For Productivity 142
Chapter Three: Igniting Your Willpower **146**
   What to know about willpower? 146
   10 Powerful Strategies To Increase Willpower 146
   12 Genius Tricks To Feel Instantly Motivated 149
   15 Inspirational Quotes That Will Fire You Up 154
Chapter Four: Your Daily Dose Of Self-Discipline **156**
   10 Expert Tips For Developing Strong Self-Discipline 157
   7 Daily Practices To Keep Building Self-Discipline 161
   20 Positive Affirmations To Inspire Self-Discipline 164
Chapter Five: Finding Focus **166**
   10 Attention Exercises To Build Concentration 166
   5 Mindfulness Exercises To Build Focus 168
   10 Ways To Conquer Distractions 170

7 Foods That Can Help Boost Your Brainpower 172

Chapter Six: Defeating Bad Habits 175

   12 BAD HABITS THAT ARE KILLING YOUR PRODUCTIVITY 175

   6 Ways To Eliminate Bad Habits Now 179

   6 Ways To Create Great Habits That Stick 184

Chapter Seven: Taming The Mind 187

   12 Essential Tips To Stop Overthinking And Control Your Mind 188

   7 Techniques To Conquer The Fear Of Failure 191

   6 Secrets For Creating A Success Mindset 194

Chapter 8: Planing For Your Success 197

   6 Techniques To Succeed At Goal Setting 197

   5 Less-Known Goal-Setting Tips Straight From The Experts.... 199

   7 Important Steps To Plan For Success 205

30 Day Step-By-Step Plan To Help You Build Habits And Fire Up Your Productivity 208

Conclusion 220

Introduction

Success and failure in life can be traced to one nurtured habit or the other. The things that make up your daily activities, the little mechanisms upon which your life runs, will ultimately determine how much you end up achieving. Habits build up into a daily routine, and these routines run our lives. All of these habits have been formed over time, through constant and dedicated practice. In this modern age, procrastination has become embedded into our DNA. The habit of procrastination has robbed most people of overwhelming success in life while enticing them with short-term feel-good rewards for just living the moment. Procrastination is a dream killer; a slow poison that dries up your zeal to achieve and leaves you wallowing in mediocrity. Procrastination is every promise you made to yourself but ended up breaking. Procrastination is when you let the goals you have slide due to lack of motivation. Procrastination is the roadblock that hindered you from reaching the place you had envisioned to be in five years ago.

Procrastination, even in its simplicity, is complex. Don't be deceived. In this book, I am going to unpack and dismantle the concept of procrastination. To enable you to tackle procrastination, you will need to understand the mechanism on which it works. Once the mechanism is fully understood, then techniques can be put in place to disrupt the mechanism. Throughout the chapters of this book, I will reveal to you various tricks and tactics used by the most productive people to overcome procrastination. I will be teaching you how to make good use of your willpower and stay motivated throughout the process. I only need you to believe that procrastination can be conquered and you will see yourself working to overcome it.

I am a self-help instructor with over five years of experience in helping people overcome the greatest hindrances to success. Through the years, I've noticed that the most subtle and dangerous obstacle has been procrastination. Clients walk up to me and complain about how they have put all success habits in place but have not achieved success. They seem to forget the place of time, which is a very crucial ingredient to success. Preparing for an exam a month before and two days before will not produce the same results. The reason for the latter is primarily due to a procrastinating mindset. This is why I decided to write the book to help people identify the bugs of procrastination clogging their lifestyle.

Now! Only a few people understand the power of that single word. Now encapsulates the present, the process of maximizing today. Everyday opportunities present themselves in deceptive manners. Some are quickly identified, and others would take the third eye to catch. However, catching these opportunities is one thing, maximizing them in that same instant they are found is another. Once procrastination is subdued, you instantly begin to reap the benefits in the now. Getting rid of procrastination is simply getting rid of weights that hold you back from acting when you know you should take action. Every opportunity seeping past you or ideas dangling in your head is tied to a deadline. Once the deadline is missed, the overwhelming success attached to that opportunity has been forfeited. And sometimes we won't ever come across such opportunities ever again. I am sure that sounds like that has once happened to you. Don't worry. You will learn to conquer it soon.

Each new day for me comes with a fresh testimony from somebody who has taken time to listen and apply some of the techniques I put into their hand. I receive calls from time to time from people who are glad they attended one seminar or another that I have given in the past. Their testimonies are wide-ranging and vast, covering a range of professions that had once proven to be stagnant before they were revived with the techniques I have been teaching. I discovered that the testimonies are somehow becoming overwhelming, and the testifiers were pressuring me to deliver more and more of my techniques. That is where the vision for this book came along. My main aim was to document as much as I could in one compilation so that these principles can go to places I might never be able to reach and continue the wonders they have been performing.

I have written this book in a simple style to so as not to alienate any of my readers. The techniques will be presented to you, the reader, in such a way that they can be easily followed and practiced. There are dozens of other titles out there that will only criticize you for procrastinating but will never provide you with enough information to counter your procrastination problem. There are little things that can be identified and worked on to give you the best experience while pursuing your goals. Did you know that a factor as negligible as dieting can affect how much you procrastinate? Of course, you will never hear that anywhere else. Just stick with me for this experience.

Some people have spent years procrastinating on the action to stop themselves from procrastination. In essence, they are just procrastinating on a miracle in their lives, the change that could take them to the next level. The great author, Paulo Coelho, said, "One day you will wake, and there won't be any more time to do the things you have always wanted to do. Do it now!" The subject of death is a sacred and greatly feared topic, yet it is so important. That said, you should keep in mind that every single day is drawing you closer to your death. If you don't start to change your life right now and get rid of procrastination, you will soon look back and have a trail of regrets following behind you.

I have heard people say that ideas rule the world. I beg to differ. In my opinion, it is ideas with the corresponding action that rules the world. Any life devoid of action is a life devoid of results, and what is a life worth living when there are no results to show for? Nothing in this book will be worth reading if you are not ready to apply the laid down principles that will be dished out to you. Your mind will continue to trick you into procrastinating on the change process, but it is up to you to conquer those mental roadblocks and take action. I will be stocking your arsenal with the weapons needed to bring down the enemy holding you back from reaching your full potential.

Chapter One: Beating Laziness

Laziness can go by different names at different times. Some refer to it as slothfulness, others call it idleness or a lackadaisical state of mind. But whatever the name is, we can all agree that laziness in any form is an undesirable trait that can rob you of success. Laziness is a state of mind, a psychological problem. You can refer to laziness as the unwillingness to use up stored energy. Or it can be said to be an unwillingness to undertake a task that you feel is difficult, boring, or time-consuming. Naturally human is laziness, and it takes an extra effort to overcome this innate nature and actually get things done. It is naturally easier to lie down all day long and get nothing done, to forfeit your goals and just watch time rush by. It seems like we humans are simply conditioned to live in mediocrity, to stay comfortable with anything that doesn't challenge our existence or survival. And this is the root of laziness, the foundation on which procrastination exists.

From a young age, the human body has always been bent on instant gratification. But truth be told, your dreams and aspirations will take time before they come to fruition. Allowing laziness become the order of the day will have you watching the seeds you have planted over time dry up before your face. Relating this to our present age, we seek people who absolutely live for nothing. Nothing inspires them, moves them to achieve more, or to do more to change their world. We see people who have accepted life simply for what it is. Technological advancements and changes in society has helped to facilitate the "Laziness Cause" even further. We now exist in a world where you can stay home all day and have everything brought to your doorsteps—your meals, your laundry, your groceries, etc. So, the question remains, "Why work, when everything can be done for you?"

Laziness and Your Goals

Of course, you can get comfortable with laziness and live the rest of your life bothering about nothing. Fact is, you will end up in mediocrity and with no tangible achievements to boast about. But if you are the kind of person that actually lives for something, that has a plan to outgrow their present level and become a success story that family and friends will want to identify with, then laziness is not an option.

One reason people are not motivated to work is that they can't see the beauty behind the achievement of long-term goals. Your laziness exists simply because you are uncomfortable with your present state. Once you make up your mind to leave your present state and enter the next phase of life, laziness begins to shake in its boots knowing that it is about to be knocked off. That is what you should do now. Don't procrastinate the elimination of laziness from your life. The more you postpone the action you need to take, the longer it takes before your dream come to fulfillment.

7 Tactics To Beat Laziness

Nobody likes being lazy. That is a funny truth. Most people who have discovered traits of laziness in their everyday life are not fully about the situation. The painful part is that figuring out what to do about laziness is hard. Think about your life at the moment: What are those things you would love to improve upon, ranging from family relationships, career prospects or financial status? All of these things are achievable; they can be improved upon to produce enviable results. There are tactics that can be implemented to help you overcome laziness in this regard and come out with overwhelming success. Let's study some of them:

1. **Have a clearly-defined strategy**

Laziness can't even be overcome if you haven't put down a strategy to go about achieving a particular goal. Say you want to get out of bed in the morning and achieve something for the day. You will need to have a list of actions set up for the day to help you identify where you should start with. In fact, having a well-structured strategy is already halfway to defeating laziness. The important question here will be: What is it that I want and how am I going to do it? Have a brainstorm session and identify ways of achieving your goals. Where do you need to go? Who do you need to talk to? How are you going to do one thing or the other? Write them down from the beginning of the process to the end. One thing you will notice as you put down your plans is that the joy of seeing them accomplished will come over you. That a step in the right direction.

2.   **Be self-aware**

Laziness is a stealthy beast. You need know when it is around. Or maybe you know but you just can't do anything about it. One way to tackle laziness is the ability to identify what your laziness is. Laziness for you might be sitting through hundreds of Netflix movies all day and getting nothing done, but that is not laziness for a movie analyst or critic who gets paid to watch and rate movies. Other people can spend hours in a bathtub filled with bubbles and sipping red wine from a wine glass. That can be seen as relaxation, but at some point, it becomes outright laziness. Know how to identify when your relaxation has gradually slipped into laziness. Once you have been able to identify the presence of laziness, then it will be easier for you to fight it.

3.   **Learn to love the things you do**

If you dislike an activity, the urge to do it will forever be missing. Sometimes, people aren't lazy, but they are not motivated to perform a certain task, and that results in "laziness." There are straight-A students who will procrastinate on writing their English essays because they hate writing, but they can spend hours and hours in calculus operations. Now these students not necessarily lazy, but writing essays is not something they enjoy. Although they might end up producing wonderful essays, the motivation to start was lacking, and this caused them to procrastinate.

Learning to appreciate whatever you need to do is a skill that needs to be developed over time. It might be a slow or gradual process, but in the end, it will surely pay off. Acquiring the right mindset will definitely have a drastic effect on how much you get done.

4. **Set a timeframe**

It could range from 10 minutes to one hour, and in this period tell yourself that there will be no break until you have carried out that task. You have thesis work to type? Sit behind your computer and type for the next ten minutes and see how far you can go with that. Set an alarm to gauge how much you can get done within that timeframe. Usually, your mind will immediately be conditioned to keep going after that task. In fact, your mind might become excited about the next challenge, seeing how much it has been able to accomplish within ten minutes. Once you get involved with the process, it is quite tempting to stop. After conquering the 10-minute challenge, you can then go further and keep pushing yourself. Go for a 30-minute benchmark and see how you fare. Then go for an hour, and so on. But remember that discipline is the key here. If you are failing at staying put for 10 minutes, there is a good chance that you will not succeed at 30 minutes. So, before you go any further, ensure that your body now understands what it means to sit and work for 10 minutes.

5. **Shut down any escape route for the time being**

What are those things that can constitute distractions for you and cause you to get lazy and procrastinate? Ask yourself: Where do I always escape to whenever I am not willing to work? Could it be a book, or a video game, or even Instagram? Whatever it is, it should be removed and taken far from you. Uninstall those apps if need be. Lock up those game pads in a drawer if need be. Do these things until you have achieved something worth achieving.

6.   **Scold yourself**

When there is no one else to check on your excesses, you have to do that for yourself. When you no longer stay with your parents or someone older than you who can shout you out of bed, you should be able to do that for yourself. Remember that your body and mind are built to serve you, and they become quite dormant when allowed to do so. Get strict with your own self. You might call it discipline, but that word has been overused and has little value. Give yourself a talking to and say the things that you are scared to tell your own self. That way, your mind will understand that you aren't playing around anymore.

7.   **See the benefits**

There is always something in store for you whenever you perform a task. Identify these benefits and brood over them. Take some time to appreciate them and see a future where they have all been accomplished successfully. Imagine the adventures you could possibly encounter by just beating laziness and taking that first step. Of course, there will be difficulties, obstacles and the like, but don't fixate on those. They will only discourage and help ruin the moment.

10 Essential Energy-Boosting Foods

A lot of people notice that they easily get tired, even after performing small activities at some point during the day. We have all been there at one point or another. It's 12 PM and you already notice that you can't drag your body off a chair. Your body suddenly become heavier. Taking in just any kind of food during this time does not help the situation. Keep in mind that food items that are high in fat and calories will leave you more fatigued than you were before eating them. They usually require more energy to digest.

Lack of energy can drastically affect your performance and your willingness to work. The truth is that the quantity and quality of food you eat can greatly affect your energy levels throughout the day. There are a variety of foods that are known to give energy, but only a handful of these contain the essential nutrients needed to increase the energy levels and keep you alert throughout the day. Foods like sugar or refined carbs can give quick jolts of energy that die within hours. But the body needs energy that is more sustainable, and this can only come from a well-planned diet. Work these following examples into your meals and see the wonder they will work in helping you combat laziness.

1.   Brown Rice

This not the first food that might come to mind as per energy provision, but brown rice does wonders. Unlike white rice, brown rice is less processed and retains more nutritional value in the form of fiber. Brown rice is very rich in manganese, and it converts protein and carbs into fuel to energize the brain and body. This food released energy slowly and steadily throughout the day, helping to keep you motivated and alert. Brown rice can be served with vegetables to enhance its energy provision function.

2.   Sweet Potatoes

Apart from their almost sugary taste, sweet potatoes are also very good energy boosters. They are very high in carbohydrates, beta-carotene (Vitamin A) and vitamin C which will keep fatigue at bay throughout the day. A small-sized sweet potato could contain about 22 grams of carbohydrates, 28% of the RDI (Reference Daily Intake) for manganese and an impressive 438% of the RDI for Vitamin A. The body digests sweet potatoes at a very slow pace thereby providing you with a steady supply of energy. Sweet potatoes can either be fried or boiled and taken with tomato sauce.

3. Bananas

Bananas are composed mostly of sugars such as glucose, fructose and sucrose. They also have some quantity of fiber in them. Bananas are a very good source of carbohydrates, potassium and vitamin B6, all known to provide the body with steady energy. Have a banana with peanut for a well-rounded snack, or throw slices of them into your morning cereal and watch yourself stay energized throughout the day.

4. Honey

A spoonful of honey is as powerful as half a cup full of energy drink. Honey usually acts as a time-released muscle fuel during exercise and it helps to replenish muscles after a workout session.

5. Eggs

A single egg contains about 70 calories in all, plus another 6 grams of proteins. Leucine, an amino acid present in eggs, helps cells take in more blood sugar, stimulate the production of energy in the cells and increase the breakdown of fat to produce energy. The energy released from an egg meal is provided very slowly for the body to utilize. Eggs are also very rich in B vitamins that help enzymes perform their roles in the food breakdown process. Eggs are also known to contain more nutrients in one calorie than most other foods. These nutrients can help to keep the hunger away for a long period of time. You can have your eggs scrambled, boiled, fried, or as an omelet.

6. Beans

Beans are very high in protein, and conventionally proteins are not believed to provide energy. But that is a wrong belief. Beans are a great source of energy, especially if you are a vegetarian. It contains a lot of fiber which slows down digestion. It is also rich in magnesium that directly supplies your cells with energy.

7. Coffee

Coffee provides you with that early morning jolt needed to get you alert and prepared for the day's activities. It works, and that is why a lot of people have a cup of coffee every morning to start their day. Coffee is high in caffeine which passes quickly from your bloodstream over to your brain where it inhibits the activity of adenosine, a neurotransmitter that quiets the central nervous system. But it should not be abused. When taken in excess, it can get you jittery and interfere with your sleep.

8. Dark Chocolate

This one rings strange, right? Let me explain. Dark chocolate contains more cocoa content than normal milk chocolate or any other form of chocolate. It contains antioxidants that assist in blood flow around the body thereby aiding the spread of energy. Because of this, oxygen is delivered more effectively to the brain and muscles. Also, the increased blood flow caused by these antioxidants also helps to reduce mental fatigue and help the mood.

9. Avocados

They are highly rich in healthy fats and fiber. The fats help to facilitate blood fat levels and encourage the absorption of nutrients from the bloodstream. They are also stored up in the body and used up for energy when it is necessary. The fiber in avocados, which accounts for about 80% of the whole content, can help to maintain steady energy flow around the body. Avocados also contain a lot of B Vitamins which are required if the cell mitochondria will perform optimally.

10. Nuts

Walnuts and almonds are noted to contain enough omega-3 and omega-6 fatty acids, and antioxidants which can increase energy levels and distribution in the bloodstream. Nuts have high calories, proteins, carbs and fats. All of these are nutrients that nuts release slowly throughout the day keeping you energized. Vitamins and minerals such as manganese, iron and vitamin E are some of the treasures that can be found in nuts. All of these give little jolts of energy in their own small ways.

5 Tricks To Get Energized And Stay Energized

Staying energized throughout the day is one sure way to get hold of laziness and prevent procrastination. The energy that is referred to here can be mental energy, physical energy or psychological energy. A deficiency in any of the following of them can cause a slowdown of the other bodily process. In our world today, it is commonplace to find out that you have totally become zapped of energy and you have lost your zest for life. Nothing breeds procrastination more than that. If you discover that you suddenly lack energy to carry on, then there are a lot of tricks you can use to snap out of it.

1. **Do something fun**

This one can help you deal with mental stress. The brain is a fun-loving sense organ that hates monotony and boredom. Once you have kept on with one task for so long and the brain gets tired performing the task, the zeal to return to it a second time and perform that task will never be there. Because the brain will dread that moment. Pause for a while and get your brain to do something different. Pick up your cat and stroke its fur. Play a little hide-and-seek with the dog. Listen to music while you work. Make sure you add a little fun to whatever it is you are doing, but you will want to make sure that you don't become distracted. After some time, you should get back to work.

2. **Take a short power nap**

Avoid the temptation to keep working and ignore the tiredness and stress. You are not a machine, and even machines themselves rest. Once you feel drowsiness coming over you, take out a few minutes and have some sleep. You can just bow your head on your table replenish your mind and alertness. If only you can understand the wonder of a short nap. It is like rebooting a system. Everything comes out new and refreshed, ready for a new phase.

3.   **Go outside**

Get some sunlight and fresh air. Your body itself is always yearning for a new environment from time to time. If you have been in an office with air conditioning for hours at a time, it is time for you to go breathe some fresh air somewhere more natural. Walk to a park and watch the scenery. Observe the children playing with their pets and smile a little. Who knows, you might get inspired for next art project.

4.   **Play mind games**

Get your brain and mind to work. Their dormancy might be the reason for your lack of energy. Do something that will challenge your mind, brain, and thought patterns. Read an article from the internet or a short story from a book. Play chess with your computer. Brainstorm with your colleagues. All of these things get your brain going and your body will instantly follow suit.

5.   **Reduce your workload**

One major reason for fatigue and energy loss is size of workload. With a large workload you either get plenty things done badly or you get only a few done correctly. Streamline your daily activities so that stress can be controlled. Pay more attention to the most important activities. Then consider getting help from if you feel it is necessary.

Chapter Two: Powering Up Productivity

Productivity is the direct opposite of laziness. Once laziness has been successfully conquered, productivity comes next. Productivity requires a step-by-step approach for it to be achieved. It isn't just a one-off activity. That is why it is necessary to put systems in place to get things done when they should be done. This system will define your way of doing things, your methods, and processes. These systems can be developed, or they can be learned. In this chapter, I am going to reveal to you some systems that can help you get things done and become more productive.

Getting Things Done (GTD)

GTD is an effective way to organize and track your tasks and projects. The main aim of the GTD method of productivity is to ensure a 100% trust in a system for collecting tasks and ideas and plans. The GTD provides you with a way to track what you need to do per time and how you need to do it. Once the GTD system is in place, the amount of stress that you will go through trying to remember all the things that should be continuously done will be greatly reduced. Time is also saved in the long run. The GTD works by keeping lists with a paper and a pen. The main lists you will have to make with the GTD method include:

1. In

The In list contains all of your main ideas and action points as they occur to you. Just jot them down as they come to you and ensure that you miss not a single thing. You can use a notepad and a pen for this or an app on your phone. Just go with whatever works for you. What is important is that you miss nothing as they come.

2. Next Action

This list contains all of the possible actions you may want to take in the near future. From this list, you will pick out what you will need to do next when you are less busy.

3. Waiting For

The items on this list are those that have you anticipating for something to happen. Let's say you have assigned a task to someone and awaiting their reply. The waiting list is the perfect list to put that down. Write that down with a current date so you can keep track of the person's progress.

4. Projects

A project in this regard refers to any task that requires more than one action to get it done. All of these tasks should fall into your project lists. You can make it more interesting by writing down the details of each project so that it can be used as a guide.

On top of these lists, you might need a small calendar to keep track of time-sensitive tasks and events.

Zen To Done Method (ZTD)

The Zen to Done method was specifically developed by productivity strategist Leo Babauta to help individuals build habits in a step by step manner while working through a workflow management system. The ZTD teaches one to form one positive habit after another. It makes the whole process a lot easier when these things are tackled in this manner. Some people have found out that they perform better using the ZTD method over the GTD method. The key here is to find which of them works best for you. There are ten habits that should be adopted one at a time over the course of thirty days. Experiment with them until you notice changes in your habit pattern.

1. **Collect**
   Record your ideas into a book or a notepad. Write down ay tasks, ideas, or projects that may come to your mind at any point in time. This is different from the GTD style because the ZTD mandates you to carry a simpler tool such as a notebook or a stack of cards, which are easier to carry about.

2. **Process**
   Don't allow things to pile up and fuel your procrastination. Process your email, voicemails, etc. Put a decision on all of those items as you work: delete, delegate, file it, or do it later.

3. **Plan**
   Set out the things you wish to achieve each week. Ensure that each day is a step forward towards achieving that big project for the week. Be sure to achieve something daily.

4. **Do**
   Eliminate all distractions and get to it. Declutter your work desk and your mind so that you can have even more focus.

With the distraction out of the way, set a timer and focus on the task for as long as possible. Don't try to multitask.

5. **Use streamlined lists and tools**
   Keep your lists as simple as possible. Don't allow the tools used in ZTD distract you from achieving productivity. Don't get caught struggling with the tools. Soon, you might find that the system has become too complicated for you to go on with it.

6. **Stay organized**
   Everything that belongs to you must belong to a space in your home. Once you are done using an item, it should be returned to that space. Create an organized system that works and helps you keep track of your items. Treat the organization habit like any other habit that should be developed and work towards developing it. Within 30 days there will be splendid results.

7. **Do a weekly review**
   Select a few of the long-term goals that you would love to focus on and accomplish with a space of six months to one year. Choosing many goals will only leave you overwhelmed without any tangible success. Break down a long-term goal into medium-term goals that will take a shorter time to accomplish. Create short-term weekly goals for each of these other goals. Each week, make a review of how far you have come in accomplishing that short-term goal during the week.

8. **Simplify**
   Your goals should be reduced to the essentials. Do a short review of all of your tasks and projects and find if you can simplify them. Even as you simply them, make sure that they

align to the ultimate yearly goals so that you don't find yourself derailing slowly. Select only the stuff that matter.

9. **Set a routine and follow it**
Build and develop routines that matter. Some these can include meditating, going for a walk each morning or reading at least a page each day. These routines can be developed for different times of the day, be it evening, morning, or afternoon. Also, develop a daily routine for different days of the week.

10. **Run with your passion**
This last one is very important. If you are passionate about your work, the urge to procrastinate doing them will be greatly reduced or quenched totally. Constantly seek things that you are passionate about and pursue them for the greater good. If possible, make a career out of practicing them. Having such a list will give you the fulfillment that you crave as you accomplish each of those tasks and projects.

8 Productivity Apps You Need In Your Life Right Now

A productivity app is a software that makes your job easier and helps you gets things done in lesser. With the help of faster processors and wider connectivity, our smartphones have become some form of personal assistants to us. If you are aiming to improve your productivity level, some of the apps listed below should be at the top of your list. Each year, more and more of these apps are released, providing new and improved ways of staying on track of activities. Here are some of the essential apps that can boost productivity.

1. **ToDoList**

This app has been downloaded more than 7 million times from various app store platforms. All you need to do is pen down everything you need that you need to get done, and the app goes ahead to interpret and categorize all of your tasks based on the entries. The apps help you and your team stay on track while planning projects, discussing the details, and monitoring deadlines. The app goes for $36 per year for a premium version and $60 a year for full access to your entire team.

2. TeamViewer

This amazing app allows you access to all of your remote devices no matter where you are viewing them from. You can be in one place, and the app instantly connects to the files you need that is currently located somewhere else. The connection also goes as far as giving you the leverage to hold audio meetings, video chats, and file-sharing options. With all of these features, collaboration with a wider variety of people becomes easier, and things get done faster. The app is available for iOS users and Android users.

3. Yelling Mom

Yelling Mom is a fun app to use. It works on the principles of a nagging mother who won't allow you breathing space until you have done what she told you to do. Once you schedule a task, the app goes to remind you about the task before the deadline is over by making use of some annoying alerts like a wailing siren or a referee's whistle.

4. Serene

Serene is designed specifically to handle distractions and help you give more concentration to the things that need to be achieved for that day. The app is currently in a private beta stage, and you will need an invite to be able to use it. But it is worth keeping an eye on for the meantime.

Once you have set up your goal for the day, you will be required to break them down into smaller sessions which will last about 30 to 60 minutes each. Set a timeframe that will be long enough to complete the goal. Once a session starts, the app blocks out any app that might turn out to be a distraction. A countdown appears on the screen while you work, and there is an option to play soothing music as you work.

5. Coach.me

Coach.me is a platform that connects you with online coaches who will help you achieve your goals. You will find different coaches who are specialists in different categories you can choose from. The coaching is done by email, and it is beautiful because you get to meet somebody and make a friend as you change your habits. The coaches will reply to any questions you have.

6. Loop

Loop is an Android-only app, and it employs a rather different approach to helping you concentrate on tasks. Loop is a habit-building app. Instead of getting you away from bad habits, it helps you form new and beneficial ones. Whatever it is that you should invest more time doing, Loop will help you to do it. The major features of this app include

- setting a target for things that you invest more time doing
- Provide a score for how well you are performing in developing new habits
- Set reminders to energize you when laziness sets in

7. HelloSign

HelloSign takes away the trouble involved in signing a large number of documents by giving an option to sign them electronically. All documents that are signed through this app are legally binding because the signature remains real and not electronically engineered. An extra benefit is that all documents signed through the app are all organized so that you don't have to waste time sorting through them whenever you may need them.

8. Drafts

Note-taking and journaling just became easier with the Drafts app. Once a new entry is made, the app quickly tags them and sorts them out. You can use some of the tools in the app to convert your notes to emails, tweets, emails, or documents.

12 Morning Routine Habits For Productivity

A good morning always results in a good day. And your morning routine seems to really be a major factor that sets the tone for the rest of the day. The success of your day is dependent on the very little details of your morning. You have to understand yourself and the way in which your body works to be able to grasp the full potential of your morning routine fully.

Morning routines have been proven to help some of the most successful people on the planet to achieve their goals. Once productivity is missed in the morning, it is always hard to capture at any other point during the day. Here, we will study some simple morning routine that will help you boost your productivity during the day.

1. Wake up naturally

For one person, 4 AM the perfect time to wake up and start up the day. For another person, a perfect day starts up at 6 AM. The 6 AM person isn't necessarily for waking up some hours later. Take your time to get up from the bed. I am not preaching laziness here, but there are some times that the body itself still needs to gather itself out of bed. Forcing out of bed is one sure way to create chaos. The most important thing is to get your body in tune. Some people function better during nighttime, and they end getting up late from the bed. They have been productive for that day at least. Only make sure that your body stays alert when it is time for it to produce. Resting your mind and brain long in bed is better than staying out of bed and nodding off throughout the process. You will get nothing done right that way.

2. Don't make major decisions in the morning

It is better that you spend the evening before writing down ideas and preparing for the next day. The willpower to make good choices and decisions is greatly reduced in the morning, and it can slow down your brain from performing at an optimum level. Once you have your day all planned out form the night before, it will help your mind to immediately get settled and get to work on the day's activities.

3. Start your day with exercise

You might have heard this about a thousand times, but the importance of exercise to your body cannot be overemphasized. Your body is begging you to train it and let off some steam. People who exercise first thing during a workday are generally known to possess more energy for the day than others. You don't have to visit a gym. You can walk to the train station, skip a hundred times, or do something else that stretches your body.

4. Clean and declutter your workspace

An uncluttered workspace will give you more concentration and productivity. Once everything is disorganized, your ability to perform optimally is reduced. People who work in a clean and organized environment are generally more productive than others who are comfortable with clutter. Clutter takes your time because your work items will be easily misplaced.

5. Complete the hardest and most tedious tasks in the morning

One beautiful thing about the morning is that your mind is as clear as possible. Your internal environment is serene and ready to perform for the day. You should prioritize this opportunity and get things down, especially those things that matter to you. Settle all of those things before your emails start jumping in, and the calls start coming. Once you clear off those tasks, the rest of the day will go on more smoothly.

6. Have a glass of cold water

Hydration helps to bring your body alive. For the whole of the time you slept, your body stayed with freshwater entering the system. Once you take water into your system, it gets your muscles going and provides your body with new energy for the day. One of the biggest indicators of low energy is a dehydrated body. Start your morning refreshed by taking a full glass of pure cold water and observe the wonders it will do for your body.

7. Reduce your screen time

Except if you make your money online or you are an online personality that needs to keep fans updated in real time, then you should keep your phone out of reach in the mornings. Smartphones and social media have been revealed to be some of the biggest killers of productivity and facilitators of procrastination. You can decide to leave your phone in its drawer until lunchtime or put it into airplane mode.

8. Meditate

Meditation will help you tackle stress and anxiety emanating from the previous day. It is best done in the early morning when the world around you is quiet, and your mind is peaceful. Meditation helps you focus your concentration and complete one task at a time, instead of getting pulled over to different tasks. It enables you to stay present in the moment.

9. Streamline your decisions

The morning time comes with a lot of choices: what to wear, where to go, who to call, what to cook, etc. Work on these decisions so that they don't too much of your time each morning and cause you 'decision fatigue.' Have a routine for your morning, such as what to wear and what to eat. Make it simple so that the decision is made quickly and you can go on with your life.

10. Be grateful

Wake up each morning and acknowledge the good things in your life, no matter how small they may be. Take some minutes and practice gratitude. The process is rewarding, and it will provide you with a clearer vision for the day. It will also help you conquer negativity which is one of the hindrances to creativity and productivity.

11. Read a page or two

While exercise sets your body in motion, reading sets your mind into action. People who read are likely to stay ahead of those who do not read. Reading keeps you updated on the latest opportunities available to you and how you can maximize them.

12. Spend time with family

No matter how small it is, this is necessary. Talk to your kids. Laugh with your spouse and get them prepared for the day. A person who leaves home happy is more likely to participate better at work. The genuine happiness from know that joy exists in your family is enough to energize you for the day.

Chapter Three: Igniting Your Willpower

What to know about willpower?

Willpower is the ability to be able to control yourself; but it also goes just beyond ability as it sounds. It is a combination of will and power. Having to do something regular, relaxed, and pleasurable may not task your willpower. Often, your willpower is relaxed in the face of accessible decisions and tasks. The firm determination to do things that are difficult (such as wanting to lose weight or quit drinking alcohol) is the true definition of willpower.

Research has it that a part of your brain (the pre-frontal cortex) powers your willpower just like love and fear is being controlled by the limbic system of the temporal lobe. Willpower feeds on mental energy just like the emotions do, and this can cause you to be tired or fatigued.

I'm sure you can relate to what happens after jogging in the morning for a long time or after doing some push-ups to stay fit. Your muscles become naturally weak then. The same also applies to willpower when the part of the brain that controls it is stressed.

10 Powerful Strategies To Increase Willpower

I am about to reveal to you winning rules and tactics to help you hush up the voices that rise against your willpower.

1. Who are you?

'Man, know thyself' is a famous utterance by the philosopher Socrates. It is of the truth that you alone can tell your high and low points. There are limits to which your abilities can be stretched. You know at what points a joke becomes offensive to you.

Wanting to know yourself could bring you to ask some questions like;

- How far can I go?
- How well can I do?
- Where am I most productive?
- When and where does laziness flourish in me?

2. Self-exploration

Many a time, you face a lot of restraining factors. Most likely, you hear yourself more often than you can count make statements like "I can't go beyond here; I wasn't made for this; I can't do this anymore." The moment the "NOT" word takes center stage in most of your activities, then, you should know that your willpower is on the decline.

Go explore your abilities, push yourself to do unfamiliar feats, and challenge the status quo. In simple terms, push the limits.

3. Stand your ground

"Tomorrow, I will increase my number of sit-ups by ten." "I will start drinking just one bottle of Coke per day from next week." "I will go an extra 200 meters at the next road walk." These are probably things you said but never did. Procrastination is a huge red flag in the path of increasing willpower. The moment you stop saying and start doing is the moment you will begin to record remarkable changes. If you don't stand your ground, the statements will become a popular future recurring rhyme. So, whatever you want to do, start Now!

4. Involve your imagination

Many inventions you find today are as a result of imagination. Someone imagined having to fly in the air as a faster and more convenient mean of transportation rather than drive on the road, and it came to reality. Today, we have the most sophisticated airplanes. Same happens with willpower. The body responds to imaginations just the same way it does to experiences. If you imagined that you fail a test, you would discover that you will begin to feel uneasy, especially if you are the kind of person who detests failing. If you are having a stressed day and you imagine yourself by a pool lying in a recliner with a bottle of chill drink and the feeling of cool breeze, your body will begin to assume that position and feel relaxed. Your body feeds on your imagination. Use the power of imagination to increase your willpower.

5. Learn to say NO

Most of the challenges faced by your willpower arise from your inabilities to say no to numerous pleasures that come your way. You tend to indulge yourself in too many activities that result into nothing.

6. Have a recovery strategy

If you want to succeed in increasing your willpower, especially on a long-term basis, then you will need to consider this. Fatigue can also apply to willpower. You may find it rather hard to sustain your willpower if you go on and on so hard without any break or space to recover. It's just a matter of time before you get tired and ultimately fall back to the start. Take some short recovery breaks.

7. Be conscious of your environment

Pressure and circumstance are vital to increasing your willpower. If you want to achieve or carry out a particular task, make sure you surround yourself with related things or people. If you want to maintain stable mental health, you may as well want to hang around people who are non-toxic and not volatile with whom you can have meaningful and positive conversations. Purge your environment of people and things that tend to want to soften your willpower.

8. Do it in bits

Willpower can drown in the presence of huge tasks. It is natural to get discouraged at the sight of heavy responsibility. It could even overwhelm you. Why not break it into bits? It is more comfortable and less challenging. Deciding to read a 1000-page book a day can prove to be daunting. However, dividing the book into parts and deciding to read some pages over a specific period feels easier to accomplish.

9. Set realistic timelines

Even though you are set to increase your willpower, going overboard is not encouraged. Setting unrealistic goals is like "building your castles in the sky."

How do you keep it simple?

- Add a little more time to your reading hours
- Do five more push-ups
- Read one extra book in 2 weeks
- Doing a few more will help you record little but vital progress.

10. Understand that it is all up to you

Your decision to power up your willpower is yours. You are not in a race with anyone but yourself. Make up your mind to do this for you.

12 Genius Tricks To Feel Instantly Motivated

Motivation comes in different forms. It could come like a spark of flame (within seconds or minutes) or gradually like a highly viscous liquid (in hours or days). The good news is that you can ignite any of the two mentioned. For this particular part, here are tips on how to get motivated almost instantly.

1. Eat dopamine-releasing diet

Dopamine is a chemical released by nerve cells and is usually associated with the brain's pleasure and reward system. The release of dopamine in your body creates a feeling of pleasure which motivates you to repeat a pattern of behavior. It means that eating foods that induce the release of dopamine can increase your motivation.

Nonetheless, bear in mind that some diets are capable of reducing the release of dopamine which could cause a reduction in motivation—foods like animal fat, butter, palm oil, and coconut oil fall in this category. It is difficult to avoid these foods altogether, but you can try to reduce their intake significantly. Employ your willpower to achieve this.

2. Take a more motivating posture

In emotional intelligence (EI), mainly when dealing with empathy, nonverbal communication is critical. It is because many important things are left unsaid that being able to figure the unspoken is crucial. The same applies to motivation. Some stances, postures, and body movements can influence your confidence. In other words, it can increase or decrease motivation.

- **Sit with your chest pushed out (don't slouch)**

Sitting with your chest pushed out (a confident stance) helps you to hold your thoughts with more confidence. Alternatively, if you sit in a slouchy position or with your back curved out, it is perceived as a doubtful posture and would portray a lack of confidence.

Recent studies have shown that sitting slumped in a chair can make one feel less proud of their performance. It can also lead to people giving up quickly on demanding cognitive tasks. So, sit upright.

- **Stand straight with "arms akimbo."**

Standing at "arms akimbo" means standing with the hands placed on each hip in such a way that the elbow flairs out. It translates into taking an expansive posture, which makes the body appear more formidable and taking up more space.

It shows dominance and confidence. The scientific explanation behind this posture is that it boosts testosterone (confidence hormone) and decreases cortisol (stress hormone).

3.   Make positive pronouncements.

"I am making an exponential success," "I can do this because I was made for it," "Nothing can stop my success," "I have what it takes." Saying these things to yourself can greatly motivate you at any time and get you to perform better. Speak to yourself aloud.

4.   Make a deal

When I say the deal, I mean tell a friend about your decision and request him/her to monitor you daily to ensure you are recording improvements. Make it more practical by adding a monetary commitment to the deal.

How do I mean?

Hand over some cash to your friend on conditions that if you can achieve your motivational goal, the money will be returned to you, if not, it should be donated to the charity.

5.   Use the power of positivity to stay motivated

As long as you live, there would always be moments when negativity would set in. Sometimes, your entire day may seem to go wrong. Everything, for whatever reason, would decide to go south. Your boss at work chooses to frustrate every effort you make. Your kids could unexpectedly fall ill. Your colleagues at work appear to irritate you.

The stark truth is that we can't always control circumstances we find ourselves in, but it is our choice how we respond to them. You may find yourself in hard or unpleasant situations. Nonetheless, you will need to decide to stay motivated through them.

Here are some tips on how positivity can help you stay motivated.

- **Surround yourself with positive people**

It is said that "show me your friend, and I will tell you who you are" or you must have heard that "birds of a feather flock together." This implies that your circle of friends or association is an excellent determinant of who you are and how much you can achieve.

On the one hand, if you have around you people who are positive-minded or always optimistic even when it is hard to do so, you will most likely be influenced by their positive vibes. On the other hand, if you have a toxic or pessimistic association, you are bound to stay negative most of the time.

- **Don't dwell on things you can't control.**

There is indeed no perfect condition. Situations that are beyond your control are bound to come up. It is essential to be able to differentiate between things that are within and outside your control, rather than dwell on them or fret over them. If not, you will unnecessarily waste time on them and most likely become stunted.

6. **Have a plan (write it out)**

Do you set out for the day's activity without any ideas on how you intend your day to go? How eventually does it turn out? Do you take time to develop a schedule or plan on how you want your week to run?

It is no news that "he who fails to plan, plans to fail."

Making a plan is like having a road map to help you navigate your way into your activity for a period. It gives you a sense of direction. It also helps you cut short the time spent doing nothing or irrelevant things as well as help you enhances your productivity.

Having a plan makes you organized and gives you an inner feeling of satisfaction, especially when you can follow up on your ideas.

- Let's see how you can set up your schedule or plan for a week

- Create a list of activities you wish to carry out for the week
- Narrow the program down to a daily to-do-list
- Allocate a time range to accomplish each task
- Follow upon each task
- Check every assignment as you complete them.

7. Count your blessings and appreciate your little achievements

Once you can appreciate your little or significant achievements, you will stay motivated to achieve more. It is also important to know that forming the habit of positive reinforcement could be of great help.

Positive reinforcement is rewarding yourself for successes made or achievements recorded. For instance, after a long week of work and having achieved you set goals, you could decide to take yourself out on a treat. Buying yourself something you do not regularly buy or going to places of relaxation and recreation are good examples.

8. See from a new perspective.

If you have always had negative thoughts or feelings, you could decide to try out a new perspective of being positive. Being positive can alter your life in many ways than you can count. It is also incredibly interesting and exciting to take a positive form.

9. Try it differently

Having to repeat a routine could be tiring if it is something that would last for an extended period. Why not try it differently? Snap out of the routine. Seeing a situation or task from a different or new perspective could be quite adventurous.

10. Subscribe to motivational shows and speeches

Listening to motivational talks or reading motivational material can serve as a motivation booster. We are mostly a product of what we hear and read.

11. Go on an enjoyable and fun activity.

Sometimes, you could feel fatigued or worn out from doing the same thing over and over again. To stay motivated, you can engage in some activities that are fun and relaxing.

You could decide to listen to your favorite songs on your way to work, and you could also decide to take some time out during your break at work to stroll around. The feeling of being out of confinement is refreshing.

During the weekends, you can decide to exercise. Exercises have a way of releasing dopamine, which increases motivation.

12. Talk to someone

Sometimes, you may fail while trying to motivate yourself even after working so hard to stay positive and motivated. It is ok when you get to this point. Do not beat yourself. Instead, talk to someone you trust. It could be a family member, or you could reach out to a counselor. He/she could guide you on the best approach to return you to motivation.

15 Inspirational Quotes That Will Fire You Up

There are a thousand and one quotes that can shoot you into being motivated to do things you never thought you could. Here are some of the thought-provoking and soul-lifting quote carefully selected.

1. "If you don't build your dream, someone else will hire you to help them build theirs." —Dhirubhai Ambani
2. "Don't beg the status quo, challenge it"- Anyanwu Emmanuel

3. "Whatever the mind of man can conceive and believe, it can achieve." — Napoleon Hill
4. "Great minds discuss ideas; average minds discuss events; small minds discuss people." — Eleanor Roosevelt
5. "Have no fear of perfection – you'll never reach it." — Salvador Dalí
6. "I've failed over and over and over again in my life, and that is why I succeed." — Michael Jordan
7. "Success is most often achieved by those who don't know that failure is inevitable." — Coco Chanel
8. "Our greatest glory is not in never falling, but in rising every time, we fall." — Confucius
9. "Life is 10% what happens to me and 90% of how I react to it." — Charles Swindoll
10. "The mind is everything. What you think you become." — Buddha
11. "Start where you are. Use what you have. Do what you can." — Arthur Ashe
12. "The secret of success is to do the common things uncommonly well." — John D. Rockefeller
13. "It is hard to fail, but it is worse never to have tried to succeed." — Theodore Roosevelt
14. "Success is not final; failure is not fatal: it is the courage to continue that counts." — Winston Churchill
15. "It had long since come to my attention that people of accomplishment rarely sat back and let things happen to them. They went out and happened to things." — Leonardo da Vinci

Chapter Four: Your Daily Dose Of Self-Discipline

Our world today has literarily compelled us to some realities. And the convincing truth about this change is appalling. Think of success as one. To be successful in any job, you must have as an essential ingredient the technical skills to perform effectively. The added spice for excellence is creativity. But not everybody falls into this category. It is not because of anything; it is just that humans have not been able to set goals to achieve this. Setting goals gives you control. There is always a direction to go. It gives you an understanding of where you should start, which turns to take, and finally, your destination is secured. Some even have an idea of setting big targets, but get stuck along the process of achieving those long-term objectives.

There are different ways of achieving goals. Maintaining some goals (which may be a career, life, family, etc.) has on its strategies. This process depends on the person involved since everybody is not on the same level of achievement. Top management level personnel will have concise goals and will be very much useful in achieving it because of many years of setting goals. The experience involved will distinguish the success rate when compared to a lower management level officer.

However, with intense self-discipline, you are sure to maintain these goals effectively. Self-discipline is an essential and useful skill everyone should possess. And as important as this skill is, only a few people acknowledge its importance. Being self-disciplined does not necessarily mean you have to be too hard on yourself or express the same feeling to people around you. It does not mean you should limit your lifestyle to a boring one. The totality of self-discipline is having self-control. It is the ability to measure your inner strength and how it can be transformed to control your actions. You then have a consciousness to react without bias.

Having self-discipline enables you to carry on in decision-making, which helps you accomplish goals with ease. It is more of the inner strength to keep you going. It has control over other inner-core terrible habits. Addiction and procrastination is a deeply rooted habit which self-mastery will help eliminate. That said, it is evident that having self-discipline is necessary for our everyday life.

10 Expert Tips For Developing Strong Self-Discipline

The superb thing about self-discipline is that it is a behavior that can be learned. Our decisions are void of impulses and unsteady feelings. Here are useful tips for developing strong self-discipline.

1. Put A Date On It

Research has shown that putting dates on your activities helps you stay focused and determined to achieve them. It also helps in maintaining a regimen, which, in the long run, helps build strong self-discipline. For instance, you may attach an activity to Mondays, and consistently follow up with it. With enough time, you would have created a regimen for that activity and, in turn, have groomed self-discipline to always perform that activity on Mondays. You might think of fixing Thursdays for your karate class. Once you are committed for the first few weeks, a subconscious knowing will erupt. Even without setting reminders, you get to know that Thursdays is not for a pool party. Get a sticker and fix it on your calendar with the name of the activity. Or you can create a reminder on your mobile devices

2. Identify What Motivates You

Priority is essential in identifying how far you would be self-disciplined. Focus on the most important thing. There is no need to dabble into what will demean and destabilize you. And commitment would not set in if you are unsure of what exactly you need to do.

There is always a high possibility of success when there is a feeling of urgency. Clothe yourself with "I must" mentality. "I must always look neat, regardless of how tired I get."

You need motivation to get started. Once you have prioritized your goals, attach modules that keep you going. Your goal might be to get a stable income to maintain a comfortable daily lifestyle. This goal is appropriate and specific. Once you identify that a steady income is essential, it will help you focus on your goals. With this realized, you can control yourself against other things that might have a negative effect on your income. Understand also that you can't be self-disciplined if you are not motivated to continue.

3. Affirm your goals and visualize the benefits you would gain

There should be a plan to achieve your set targets. Most times, we get distracted by the result that we neglect the strategies to make them work.

Analyze how you think this will work well for you. Make sure you are specific as much as possible. Outlined benefits will give you a sense of accountability. Imagine you have highlighted that one of the benefits of eating healthy is good body shape. The moment you start feeding well, and you notice the change in your body, you could quickly tick the benefits as the one you have achieved already. It will push you to a place where you will embrace other interests you have discovered.

Consistently affirm your goals and the benefits you would gain from them. Your mind will repeatedly get in tune with those set targets. If you say every morning, "I am a great athlete because I'll break the record to get a $4,000 scholarship," "I am getting that contract, and it makes me a better engineer." With time, your mind becomes disciplined and determined to achieve these goals.

4. Make Achievable Plans And Stick To Them

Temptations are bound to arise whenever you are determined to achieve a goal. It might be a distraction from social networks or even your friends. Some might also come when it seems you are not making progress. You will understand that this could hinder you from actualizing your targets. However, your goals must be attainable. Don't be ambiguous. Let it be profound to your taste, work condition, lifestyle, and routine. Include precise quantity, time, people, and dates. These variables make it easy to stick to your laid-down formula.

5. Make Your Regimen A Combination Of Things You Need To Do And Things You Want To Do

Management science research has shown that combining these two activities helps form good habits and also helps you quickly achieve the needed. You can get things done, even in the fun of doing other things. Just decide on what can be combined to give you the desired result. For instance, you want to have a girl's day out to talk and have fun. You can choose the same day you have set out for the gym. After some teasing, agree with your friends to go for a workout session. You can even make it competitive. That way, you have achieved an activity you need by combining it with an event you want.

6. Sleep And Eat Well

Lack of proper sleep and food causes the prefrontal cortex (which is responsible for self-regulation) to perform less than expected. Additionally, the ability for a person to focus when they are hungry reduces to the minimum as lack of food causes lack of sugar, which in turn weakens a person. Hunger brings in a sensation of unwillingness. It is always accompanied by tiredness. Your willpower to do anything is being affected. Thus, you are not motivated to concentrate on what you need to do. To stay focused and disciplined, make sure you eat and sleep properly.

7. Reward Every Progress

Do you remember when you were a child and your parents said they would reward you with a gift if you passed your exams? And whenever you pass, and they fulfill their promise, it is always a source of motivation for you to study more? This logic also works for building self-discipline. If you reward yourself for every progress you make, that way you stay motivated to do more, keeping your eyes on the benefits to be gained.

8. Get A Self-Disciplined Circle

External motivation is the first propeller of habit formation. Just as peer pressure can cause a person to form bad habits, having a circle of self-disciplined friends could motivate you to be self-disciplined. Just as the saying goes, "show me your friend, and I would tell you who you are." Put yourself around people who give you a sense of fulfillment. These are people who have the same belief system as you. Even when it seems you are losing willpower, you get to find strength in their resilience. You would get easily encouraged if you found out that your friends have been able to ensure mastery over a particular course you are struggling with.

9. Do It For Yourself

Self-discipline is good, but most importantly, it is best if the purpose is not biased. If you are aiming at getting more disciplined, be sure it is solely a decision made for you. That way, you would appreciate every progress you make. It doesn't mean that you can't seek professional advice or instructions from friends. It just means that you have to be truthful about your action plans without any form of prejudice.

10. Project Future Challenges

You wouldn't want to fall into self-deceit by believing that everything will work as planned. You might stumble, find out what triggered it, and resist falling into the same pit in the future. Forecast other challenges that might arise as you go on the journey of self-discipline. Think of distractions and problems. They don't have to subdue you. Create a plan to tackle it.

7 Daily Practices To Keep Building Self-Discipline

Self-discipline cannot be attained in a day. It requires consistency and perseverance, and daily practices can only build this. Commit yourself to know that the journey to maximum self-discipline is not a palatable one, but the end is always a meal to remember. Here are the daily practices you can use in building your self-discipline.

1. **The Cold Bath Test**

Everyone hates a cold bath, especially in the morning. That icy blast hitting your face when you are still trying to keep your eyes open can be pretty annoying. It requires a lot of resolution and discipline to subject yourself to that icy blast every morning. And if you can pull through it each morning, that is another step to maximum self-discipline. Prepare your mind for the fact that self-discipline wouldn't look appealing at the start. And it may even become burdensome and time-consuming as time progresses. It will require you a lot of patience and commitment, especially if it is not within your culture. But in the end, you will have more reasons to stay disciplined.

2. Daily Meditation

Sitting at a spot with your eyes closed and just listening to your breathing might appear dumb at first. But do you know that meditation is a great way to build self-mastery? Because it requires a high level of concentration for you to sit at a spot and consciously listen to your breath? Consider doing this practice every day, and you will increase the strength of self-discipline. Additionally, meditation helps clear your mind, which in turn enables you to reconnect with your inner self. Try sitting and listening to your breath every morning. After some weeks, you would have disciplined your mind to focus on your inner self and would have built your self-discipline through this exercise.

3. Identify Your Weaknesses

Every human being has weaknesses, and most of us tend to overlook them. Being disciplined means you understand your flaws, challenges, and weaknesses, yet are determined to overcome them. If you are a "glutton" but are committed to stop eating out of proportion, the first step is to acknowledge your problem. "Is it that I like to taste everything I see, or I don't get satisfied when I eat more of carbohydrates" Then, ask yourself, "how can I solve this problem?" Having acquired a solution, consciously follow up on it by having in mind the picture of the result (less weight). Admitting these flaws is the first step to overcoming them. Hence, to attain the maximum state of self-discipline, you must acknowledge that there is a need for it and the hindrances stopping you from achieving it.

4. Run Every Morning

A one-mile sprint takes about six to ten minutes and a new determination to pull through. It might appear hard to accomplish at first, but it is a useful tool for building endurance and discipline. Sprinting every morning gives you an automatic jump start for the day and enough energy to pull through it. Be sure you do it before the cold bath in other to maximize your self-discipline growth. If you are reluctant to do this alone, speak to a friend about it and both of you can get started. Ensure that your aim of running is fulfilled.

5. Make Your Bed

Everyone wants to wake up and jump off their beds and get on with their day. No one sees the need to take about two to three minutes to make their beds. Hence, it requires a lot of discipline to consciously decide to make your bed. Always convince yourself that it is necessary to fix your bed because it promotes a positive habit of neatness. The good thing is that it takes very little time. A conscious effort to do it every morning can improve your self-discipline significantly.

6. Eliminate Temptations

Temptations and distractions kill discipline. Without them, attaining maximum self-discipline is possible. However, their presence causes you to either be sluggish or give up. Every distraction or temptation is unique to each goal, and understanding them helps you eliminate them and stay on course, thereby building your self-confidence. Whenever you are tempted or discouraged, remind yourself that, "this is the best time to give my best."

Affirmations by itself will not eradicate temptations. Analyze those things that get you obsessed. Clear them and refuse to go alongside that direction. If you are trying to read, stay away from the PlayStation. Video games will not help you focus during exams. Make a schedule of when to hang out with friends if you see yourself wasting a productive moment with a close acquaintance. If you are having trouble studying an e-book on your phone because of updates of an adventure game, force close the app or uninstall it if necessary.

Let temptation be a positive reminder that you have been doing well, and this time is not the moment to give up.

7. Be Intentional About Your Goals

Getting an all-around commitment to daily targets is necessary for achieving more excellent results. You wouldn't be the best version of yourself when you have not been purposeful about your goals. Start by making it clear. Write them down. Your journal or notepad can be an excellent place to pen it down. You can as well write down any affirmations you think will motivate you to keep going.

20 Positive Affirmations To Inspire Self-Discipline

Whatever you say consistently to yourself sticks in your mind permanently. It creates a consciousness in which you work in. This is why assertions are a significant part of building self-discipline. Every day when you wake up, say these affirmations to yourself.

1. I am a fantastic person, and I am thankful for this opportunity to grow.

2. I am determined to make myself better mentally, spiritually and emotionally.

3. I must work on myself. I am doing the right thing.

4. This day is an excellent day for me, and I am going through it with a spirit of gratitude.

5. I adjust to who I am becoming: my strength motivates me, and my weaknesses are a discouragement to me. I overcome every fault. My shortcomings are turned to advantages.

6. On this day, I am intentionally defining boundaries and eliminating every form of distraction and temptation.

7. I have complete control of my time, and today I am not engaging in any bad habit.

8. I am strong and capable of becoming self-disciplined. And I would attain my maximum state of self-discipline

9. At every point in time, I know what I am expected to do, and that is what I would do.

10. I am accomplishing every task I have today. I am conscious of the benefits of living healthy. Therefore, I am guided to eat right.

11. I am giving my best at everything I do today. I prosper at the work of my hands.

12. Today, as I decide to do my daily routine, I achieve all that is set before me. I am organized and prompt in every area of my life.

13. No challenge can pull me down. I surmount every difficulty. Natural circumstances do not move me.

14. Worry will not solve my problems. Therefore, I will not be anxious about anything.

15. My imagination is active. I use my imaginative power to create excellence. My mind is open to receive new ideas. I am quick to act on positive impulse. I am motivated from within. Nothing can stop me!

16. My mind is attracted to positivity. I do not see negativity. I am making progress with giant strides.

17. I affirm that I am an advantage in my world. This is not the time to give up on myself. I am not ordinary. I am undaunted by challenges

18. I reign in life. All things work together for my good. I am strengthened and energized for victory today.

19. I am life-conscious. My body is energetic and full of vitality. There is no space for sickness, disease, infirmity, or anything that brings pain to my body.

20. Nothing can pull me down. I do not see the present temptation. I am full of benefits.

Chapter Five: Finding Focus

The average human has a short attention span that doesn't even last a mere eight minutes. Surprisingly, that is the attention span of a goldfish. Because of your digital life, this number has shrunk even further. The brain is always on the lookout for the next exciting thing happening in the environment. We are most likely to get bored because of this.

Your ability to focus and pay attention to your environment is essential to your survival. It is a skill, and you have to improve it to make it better. Focus is just like the muscular system of the body. The more it is exercised, the stronger and more substantial it becomes. The process of focus building is a mental battle that you have to partake in to better your self. Don't dwell on the idea that you are the kind of person who easily loses focus. Buying into that narrative will spell doom for you.

The question now remains, how can focus be built and developed? In an age where everything is vying for your attention and pulling you in different directions, what can be done to keep your mind at alert?

10 Attention Exercises To Build Concentration

As I mentioned before, your mind and concentration strength can be exercised to increase the value. Just like a gym instructor will dish out exercises for you to do to develop different parts of your muscular system, there are some other exercises for the mind that can be used to build your "concentration system." Remember, your success mostly depends on how well you can concentrate and capture the details that surround you. Here are some of those exercises you can do.

1. **Exercise One:** Take a book or magazine and open it to any page you may find interesting. Read up that page and understand its content. Begin to count the words on the page, one paragraph after another. As you count, take note of each

word contained in each paragraph. Try to understand their function in each sentence. Then go over and make a recount. Once you notice that you can easily count the words in the first paragraph, you can move over to the next.
2. **Exercise Two:** Count the numbers backward from 100 to 1. Make a picture of each number as you count and do this as fast as you can. Concentrate your mind on picturing the whole numbers in a line of ten. Increase your count to a range of 500 and 1000.
3. **Exercise Three:** Take an object and focus the whole of your mind on it. It could be a fruit, a toy, or any other object. Observe its components and features, the things that make up this particular object. Take note of its shape, color, size, flaws, and all. Continue to pick out all of these things and don't allow your mind to wander while you do this. Even if it does, bring back to base. Do this for three minutes at a time and continue to increase until you finally master it.
4. **Exercise Four:** The next time will be to visualize the object you have just observed. Close your eyes for a while and try to picture what you have studied for some time. How go does your mind bring back the image to you? Try to bring back all of those things that you discovered while observing the object. If your mind fails to produce a clear model, open it up for a while and observe again. Then close your eyes and see how well the image forms. Do this repeatedly until you are finally able to picture the object in its full form.
5. **Exercise Five:** Choose a particular word or phrase in your mind and keep repeating it to yourself in your mind. Do this silently without causing any attention towards yourself. Do this until your mind learns to concentrate throughout the process for about ten minutes.
6. **Exercise Six:** You can play a small game with your nose. When going through a flower garden or the local park, keep your nose open and ready to grasp the different types of flower smell that can be detected. This exercise requires some level of

concentration to differentiate the various scents in the environment.
7. **Exercise Seven:** Take a good position and stay quiet. You can either lie down flat or sit on a chair. Do not move as you remain in that position. Keep your full concentration on your heartbeat. Try to picture the mechanism of blood flow throughout your system and try to figure out where the blood reaches around your body. With constant practice, you will soon be able to feel your blood flowing through your body.
8. **Exercise Eight:** Practice the art of self-control. You might be the kind of person with a strong desire to talk and spill secrets about others. By learning to control these urges, you will be able to energize your concentration strength. To continually put these things behind your mind and force them to remind there is so much power than you can understand. It will help you put your will and desire in check. No matter how exciting the news may be, try your possible best to keep it under wraps until the appointed time for which it should be revealed.
9. **Exercise Nine:** Try to keep your mind void of any form of thought. This is probably going to be the hardest of all the other activities. Your mind is constantly being bombarded with ideas, and to keep them out requires a lot of concentration. Try to do this for one minute at a time. Once you conquer that timeframe, you can go on to five minutes and then ten minutes.
10. **Exercise Ten:** Engage in art. Art here does not only refer to painting, drawings, or sculptures. Art is a whole lot wider than that. Art is in your everyday conversation. Art is in the movies you watch and the song you listen to. Pay closer attention, and don't just do these things because you are bored. You might not know what you can discover, and you will ultimately learn concentration by paying attention to these little things.

5 Mindfulness Exercises To Build Focus

Focus is considered an essential ingredient to success in life or any endeavor. Focus is a rudiment to the improvements of your thinking mechanisms such as your learning ability, perception strength, and problem-solving. Learning to build focus becomes very important when these factors are considered. Focus helps you achieve mental clarity. There are several ways with which you can start practicing how to create focus and use it to complete any given task.

Mindfulness in this regard refers to a state of being present in the moment. It is being aware and open at the moment. Mindfulness deters your mind from wandering around and losing its place.

1. **Exercise One:** You are never your best whenever you are in a hurry. When you slow down, you learn to reconnect with the environment. Slow down as you walk through the driveway. Don't chew your food too fast. Take your mind and appreciate the world around you. Slowing down does not mean that you are sluggish or a sloth, slowing down is looking deeper and preventing mistakes. Remember what they say: Slow and steady wins the race.
2. **Exercise Two:** What do you see when you close your eyes. What lies behind your closed eyelids? The eyes are a major source of distraction to the mind. Close your eyes and cut away that distraction. Close your eyes and focus on the pictures in your mind. Listen to the sounds around you. Your other senses perform better once your eyes are close, so close them and see what you can discover.
3. **Exercise Three:** Train your eyes to catch the footprints pattern. Learning footsteps is one right way to understand human and animal nature. Footsteps are like messages that need to be deciphered. If you can train your mind and eyes to catch things as small and seemingly insignificant as footstep pattern, it will be quite easier to pick the essentials.
4. **Exercise Four:** Every time we are prone to emotions which we may not necessarily understand. We might soon find ourselves not paying attention to what we feel. This exercise involves you finding a name for your emotion and pinpointing the reason why you feel that way.

5. **Exercise Five:** Observe the people around you. You can practice in an office or in any public space. Keep your eyes on one person and note what they are doing. Observe their body language and their dress pattern. Try to keep a picture of them in your mind, so that forget them once you take your eyes away. Become more mindful of the people around you and the actions they carry out.

10 Ways To Conquer Distractions

Most of the time, we start with good intentions of having our minds on the task at hand, but something happens are we soon discover that we have lost focus. You know that you have the ability, the strength, and the drive to carry on, but distractions always have the upper hand and soon you notice that you have been overpowered. Think of distractions as small pests in your workplace that bore holes and prevent productivity. If you do nothing about them, they grow stronger and continue to build their net over you. If only you can take some time off and try to calculate how many hours you have lost to distractions, you will understand how bad the situation has become. And the truth is that distractions are so powerful, and conscious efforts needs to be made to be able to conquer them. Some of these strategies will help you stay on top and overcome distractions:

1. **Identify your sources of distraction:** Different people have different things that distract them. For some, it would be watching ballet dance videos on YouTube, while for others, it would be their own thoughts. All you need to do first is to identify what constitutes a distraction to you. This is the first step to take to eliminate these pests.
2. **Develop distraction-proof habits:** There are small habits built over time that can help you become a better person overall. For these habits to grow, first you must create a friendly environment devoid of distraction for them. It is never an easy task, and it will require a lot of work. Small things like ads block and switching off your phone can help you build

these habits. Other people around you should have an idea that you have entered a distraction-free mode and you can get them informed with simple acts like closing your office door or putting on a headphone. Put away anything that can serve as a source of distraction, and your mind will begin to learn that it can do without those distractions.
3. **Keep your mind in check:** Your thoughts are some of the most subtle sources of distractions. Watch how your mind begins to wander when you are carrying out the most serious activities, even during an exam. We spend a good percentage of our mind thinking about something else while carrying out a task. The key here is to notice when the mind is about to begin the journey and hold it back. This will mean paying a lot of attention to your mind. If there is a problem at hand that your mind keeps going back to, then you should find a solution to that problem and free your mind.
4. **Don't multitask:** Myths are flying around about the benefits of multitasking. Although some people are very proficient in the act, I do not endorse it. Multitasking is not only a distraction but a clear source of fatigue to the brain. You might feel like you have achieved more when you multitask, but when you go back, you will discover a lot of mistakes with than things that you may have thought you did right. Stopping one task and starting up another is a brain drain and focus can easily be lost.
5. **A short break will do you good:** Whenever you notice yourself getting distracted, you can take a short break and reassess the work at hand. Try to recapture the reasons why you have to remain focused on your job and give your mind a reason to concentrate. Your brain needs to be reminded about why the task at hand is important and why distractions should not even be an option.
6. **Break down the tasks into smaller fragments:** Distractions are more prone to present themselves when a project seems overwhelming. It is better for tasks to be broken down into smaller projects so that the brain is deceived into thinking the

job is easier and will take a much smaller timeframe. With each accomplished project, you fell a sense of accomplishment that drives you to do more.
7. **Set Deadlines for each task:** Don't just start up a task without a deadline. Timing is everything. Give your mind and brain a timeframe to complete the task. This will give a sense of urgency, and your mind will be eager to get the job quicker.
8. **Set yourself apart:** This one goes for people who are prone to get distracted when people are around them. It is necessary to have people around you at all times, but you should also be able to identify when they constitute a distraction in your life. Before you start up a task, you can tell the people around you about how important at hand is and how much space you would love to be given. Or you can take yourself away from them until you get the job done. They might not understand how important it may before you to complete that task successfully.
9. **Track the daily pattern of your life:** It would make sense for you to track each day's activities at night to find out how much time was spent doing what. This evaluation will quickly help you identify the distraction patterns in your life that you need to combat. When these habits have been identified, you can now start working towards creating habits that will eliminate their effect.
10. **Start early:** Earlier in this book, we talked about staying in bed until your body is ready to get up. But sometimes you need to push your body out of bed to get things done. This period of the day is best used to get your day started. There are hardly any distractions at this point, and your mind is most active and ready to perform.

7 Foods That Can Help Boost Your Brainpower

You should do everything to protect your brain and help boost its operating power. The importance of your brain cannot be overemphasized. It is in charge of a whole lot of things that go on around your body. When all of these are considered, you now discover why it is quite important to keep your brain in peak working function.

Some foods can be taken to get the brain working at its best. These foods have a lot of impact on the structure and the health of the brain. They also have some minor and major nutrients that are needed by the brain to perform to optimum levels. It has been proven over time that our body parts begin to deteriorate as we grow old, and this includes the brain, too. But even with this, you can help your brain to maintain its health as you learn to eat smarter. Some of these foods can help your brain perform better:

1. **Blueberries**

Research has shown that the flavonoids produced by this fruit are very for memory improvement. They are also known to protect the brain and reduce the effects of Alzheimer's disease and dementia. The brain also needs the antioxidants produced by the blueberries and to help improve communication among the brain cells. You can add them to your early morning cereal or squeeze out their juice.

2. **Fatty Fish**

The omega-3 fatty acids contained in fatty fish are known to reduce the quantity of beta-amyloid in the bloodstream. This beta-amyloid is a form of protein that forms lumps in blood vessels and the brain, thereby causing Alzheimer's disease. Omega-3 fatty acid also helps to increase the blood flow towards the brain. Some of these fishes include sardines, tuna, sardines, and salmon.

3. **Broccoli**

Glucosinolates contained in broccoli is broken down by the body to form isothiocyanates. These isothiocyanates are known to reduce the possibility of degenerative diseases occurring in the body. Broccoli is also very rich in flavonoids and vitamin C, which are also necessary for the brain health.

4. **Turmeric**

Curcumin contained in turmeric enters the brain to directly benefit the cells reproducing there. Curcumin is a potent antioxidant and anti-inflammatory compound that benefits memory system in the brain. Studies have also shown that it helps to improve the mood when it is taken.

5. **Whole Grains**

Whole grains are known to contain a lot of vitamins which is very important for the development of the brain and the neurological system. Whole grains include foods like barley, rice, oatmeal, and whole-grain pasta. Some of them can be taken as early cereal, or they can be boiled and taken with sauce. It is all left to your culinary imaginations.

6. **Kale**

Kale is another vegetable that contains glucosinolates, and just like broccoli they are also known to help reduce the body's susceptibility to degenerative diseases and keep the brain healthy and ready to function.

7. **Green Tea**

Caffeine, which is very important for brain function, can be found in Green tea. Taking green tea in the morning can help to give the brain a dose of alertness, memory, and focus. Another essential nutrient in green tea is L-theanine. L-theanine is an amino acid that promotes the activities of the neurotransmitter GABA. L-theanine can also help the brain relax when there has been an insanely stressful activity.

Chapter Six: Defeating Bad Habits

By now, you must have been practicing the tips given in chapters four and five about self-discipline and staying focus. Nevertheless, a conscious effort must be taken to sustain what has been learned. Thorough and sustained learning requires the learner to understand the position at which he is learning. Knowing your pace and the attitude involved is a good starting point. As it is not enough to acquire new set skills but also to identify those negative behavior pattern that ruins your productivity. These are setbacks that have been a part of your life. But what happens when you discover that the negative attitudes that frustrate your learning process are your habits? And these habits, as at when realized, have reduced the pace at which your productivity level is achieved. Our attention is not on when the bad habits started, as some began theirs at a tender age while others developed theirs as they grew into adulthood. It is a good thing that it is discovered and your statistics must have summarized the effect per time, ranging from emotional, psychological, health, etc.

Bad habits have a way of dealing with us. Some start with our inner self. It proceeds to destroy our self-image and self-worth while many others reflect on our productivity level. Whatever the effect might be, you can defeat it. You would want to know that the adverse impact of these bad habits can be so dangerous that they affect your health and mental state. And an unhealthy being can't perform to the best of his abilities.

12 BAD HABITS THAT ARE KILLING YOUR PRODUCTIVITY

1. **Trying to do every task**

Humans are not robots. And no one anticipates you to do everything. Even robots are programmed for a specific job. But more frequently than not, you tend to overwork yourself by trying out every task.

Trying something new is not bad, but doing every task is the problem. You tend to lose focus when you do that. You won't be able to boast of specialization. It would be wrong if a sales manager is seen performing the task of a personnel admin. Just as you can't eat everyone's food, so can't you do every job.

2. Letting social networks distract you

Everyone is excited at the new interface that comes with the latest update, the added filters that beautifies the sight and the one-time swipe function. And since work has taken the space of your intimate friends, getting another acquaintance who wouldn't leave anytime soon is inevitable. You then spend more of your time with them to the extent that it becomes a habit. That feeling of excitement that comes from sticking to your digital friends on the different social media platforms and the trends and updates has always been a major killer to your productive moment.

3. Clutter

You might not think of confusion as a big deal until you figure out that you can't get what you want without looking for it. Why? Because it is not organized as it ought to. An office cabinet filled with outdated reports, newspapers, and journals can add up to your work. It presents to your partner how disorganized you are. All office documents have their filing system. Littering it up with other irrelevant kinds of stuff makes everywhere untidy, and you will always need to hand yourself a search warrant.

4. Lack of a plan

Waking up into the day with the right mental attitude is good. But having no intention to fulfill the day is not a good thing to bank on. Sticking to the general plan or a plan of "no plan" is a bad habit you need to eliminate. You can't go with the flow when there is a goal to achieve. What if the general plan is not fit for your specific task?

5. Thinking of work every time

The main passion that fuels your job is the love that you have for it. But this love cannot be productive if it is not well-expressed. Thinking of work every time leaves you worried. You tend to ask yourself multiple questions at a time. What do I do next? What about the report? How do I present this paperwork? And so on. It then distracts you from creating time to plan for the work. What you have been doing is mainly anxiety.

6. First thing last, the last thing first

This sequence is a total reversal of priority. Everyone wants something, but not everyone has been able to pin their specific needs down according to how bad they need them. Generalizing what you need may not help you to do things differently. Imagine giving too many options when you can structure your needs down to the order of its importance.

7. Easy task first, hard ones later

The hard task is technically challenging, and that's why it's called that name. People tend to push the more difficult task to the future whereas, those are the most important. Getting to do the more straightforward job first, without creating a strategic plan on how to solve the harder one, pushes the task to a tight corner. It becomes harder every time it gets pushed back. Pushing an essential task to the future wouldn't make you achieve your aim. It even adds more pressure to the job.

8. Complaints

Our mental and psychological state in the workplace could be affected most times, and it is just natural for humans to get tired. And one attitude that reflects tiredness is the vocal utterance that accompanies it. Mumbling and soliloquy is a common symptom. Complaints come from a negative feeling when the right results are not achieved. And the effects of these feelings result in an unwillingness to finish the task.

9. The perfect little bit

Dedication is an attribute that shows that you value your work. This catalyst might sometimes involve adding spices to the bit that makes up perfection. Perfection is what defines our excellence. But it would be burdensome when we tend to spice up all the bits. And the bits in itself is unimportant to the result intended. What happens is that we get stuck? We get frustrated, right? Then, stress pops in.

10. Negativity

Negativity is more of a mind thing than a physical thing, the result of which is visibly assessed. It all starts with the wrong mentality to progressively have a poor outcome. Most times, it doesn't come because someone inspired it. It comes as a reminder in your mind. It allows you to blame yourself, put yourself down. You then conclude that you are not fit to meet the target or to do any extraordinary thing. What happens is that the result will be reduced.

11. Between the fence

A lot of times, we are faced with a great decision to make. These are choices that determine the progress of our success or an entirely purposed success. It might even be a concern that stems from the outside world but affects our immediate. A good example is when you are faced with a decision to execute a project with a handful of clients. Those which have different variables such as technicality, speed, experience, expertise, and so on. But no one wants to make the mistake of choosing the wrong one. However, not making one at all wouldn't complete the task. Your indecisiveness even prolongs the completion date.

12. Little time to rest

A power nap is believed to revive energy and set you up to start an excellent task. So, what happens if all you got left after a hectic day is just a little time to rest? Most times, the office job is taken home as overtime. But we tend not to get the best out of the task because our body system has not been revitalized. This routine is a nasty habit that needs a second thought.

6 Ways To Eliminate Bad Habits Now

Eliminating bad habits is a great decision to take. Some have, over time, chosen to ignore their bad habits because they consider it a proper way of life. Others have found measures to manage it. Either way, life can be lived to the fullest when you are confident that no negative attitude is eating you up. Understand that it is quite possible to eliminate bad habits, and you need to be ready to do this. The following can be employed as a guide to help you out.

1.   Getting ready

A great way to start a task is when you are fully aware of the task at hand. The same thing is with eliminating bad habits. Prepare yourself for this task. Preparing yourself means saying, "I am ready for this, and there is no better time than now." Come to the full understanding that you have signed up to do the better thing. Let it start from within you. Just like when you are inclined to think otherwise, align yourself with this new mentality that "This is my perfect time to eliminate those bad habits, and I am getting better." You might be tempted to weigh your options. Don't give it a shot. Put everything in place to get you going.

- **Think differently**

Human beings are naturally comfortable when things are easy. And for you, the bad habits must have given a bit of comfort. It's high time to think differently about the whole situation. Have a mindset that you are fighting a battle with your bad habits. Think of yourself as the soldier that is equipped with the modern-day armory and your bad habits have only stone-age weapons. With this mindset alone, you have already placed yourself in a position of victory. All other steps that will be taken will not be considered grievous.

- **Intentionality**

A deliberate attitude needs to be asserted here. You need to stand for this new movement regardless of any challenge that may accompany this exercise. Activate the power of the mind to achieve the great result of breaking those bad habits

2. The Snail Approach

If there is anything the snail is known for, it is its slowness in movement. No one is suggesting to you to get a snail (you might if you want to). But the snail approach brings an understanding that you have to start small. And starting small sometimes might appear slow. Understand that your new habit will not come as a "big bang" but in a steady-state. Your aim at this level is progress. Ensure that you are doing something different from the old habit. There is no need to rush.

3. Identify the why

You might not have thought about why you do the things you do, maybe just because it has become a part of you. Get settled and identify those things that trigger you to do what you do. Maybe you overthink your job anytime you receive a new mail. Or you actively stay on social networks whenever you have a dispute with your friend. Just identify the triggers behind those bad habits, and you have started the elimination process already.

- **Evaluate**

A sincere appraisal of your negative behavior is necessary at this stage. Sincerely weigh the consequences of these behaviors with the right one. You would agree that the positive sides far outweigh the negative. Don't crucify yourself when you have a setback. It is an expectation that is likely to happen. Ensure you get back on track

4. Create reminders

One of the first drives that support our commitment is when we are constantly reminded of it. You need to be reminded that you want to eliminate these bad habits. It will not only help you at present, but will also create an atmosphere for a great future.

- **Digital reminders**

Pushing a reminder can work well with most mobile devices. You can search for apps that create a to-do list, look up the options and enable the alarm function. Create a word or phrase that continually reminds you of the habit to break. It's quite evident that, by now, you must have identified the cause or triggers of your bad habit. If yours is staying on the social networks often, you may want to have a word that says, "it's time to sleep." Or if you are fond of negativity, you might have this: "My negative thought pattern will not help me, I deserve happiness, and that's what will work for me." Ensure you set the alarm at least 10 minutes before the beginning of your extremes. You will know when you are about getting there. This well-structured strategy will create enough time for you to adjust effectively.

- **Journaling**

Writing things out yourself will give you a sense of personalizing your target. Get a journaling book in the book store or create one for yourself. Divide the page into two vertically. Start with writing your noted terrible habits on the first side. Add reminders of what you should do (or not do) on the other side. This idea models the digital reminder. You could analyze your progress by ticking the habit you are constantly reminded of.

- **Friends**

You might consider telling your friend about this move. There is always a friend that pushes us until a task is done successfully. He/she might even come up with better suggestions or plan. This action will give you a sense of accountability. Ensure you inform your friend to provide you with a progress report, or you could come up with a guide yourself. He wouldn't want you to be ridiculed with failure. Not again!

- **Stickers**

Inscribe short words/phrases on labels and fix it around you. The little sticky note scattered around you will serve a perfect reminder of what you need to do. Ensure you attach it where your bad habit triggers. It can be in your office, on your calendar, notepad, on the wall and even in your car.

5. **Switch your surroundings**

Visiting a particular place might be the trigger to one of your bad habits. You tend to drink more bottles of beer whenever you hang out with friends at the local bar downtown. Consider going to another bar, different from the one you frequent, this time alone. Create a new atmosphere for yourself. Sometimes, the feel of a place you continuously visit pushes you to react negatively.

- **Rewarding every broken habit**

"Broken habit" here means that you have been able to stop the practice successfully. You are no longer seen doing it. Motivate your progress into positivity by rewarding yourself. Everyone needs encouragement. And this reward system may be the only thing that will keep you going till you achieve maximum success.

- **Substitute**

A meaningful way to reward yourself is to look for a positive habit that will substitute the bad habit. A habit is a part of your life. Just like the game of football, the less effective player is replaced; but in urgent cases, a dire need to change the fit player is inevitable when the strategy does not seem to work. It is the same here. Change the less productive habit to have a more productive life.

You would also agree that those bad habits come with fulfillment. Most times, it is there to fulfill a need that might come as a result of depression, sadness, rejection, failure, boredom, etc. if those needs are not met with another thing, then, there is a loophole.

- **Draft a plan and strategize**

Know what to do the when triggers immediately come up. Work with the strategy of reward system any time you replace your bad habit with the positive pattern. Don't give space for loneliness. Loneliness in this regard means dissatisfaction in your expectations. Don't expect to be in that mess again. This practice would be quite more comfortable for you when you avoid the triggers

- **Look out to the future**

The future you are looking out for is someone else's reality, and some people are doing what you want to achieve now. Why not move close to them and make new friends. If restraining yourself from your old friends will give you enough time to break off from your bad habits, you need to give it a shot.

6. **Seek professional support**

If you still find it challenging to adopt a positive attitude towards the effort of helping yourself, consider seeing a professional. The psychologist can help identify psychological, emotional, and behavioral patterns that trigger bad habits. He will ensure your progress and can be accounted to.

6 Ways To Create Great Habits That Stick

You may have wondered why your plans are not working as expected. It may have worked for some time, but it looks dull and does not seem to work. You may have told yourself to stop staying 8 hours a day on the internet without learning something new, but it seems not to work. Do not fret. Come to a new awareness that this is a different game for you. It's not the game of chance but total commitment. Be sure that you have been able to discover what triggers your bad habits and the estranging patterns behind it. You might need to analyze your pursuit and the sacrifice behind it. "What do I want and how bad do I want it to change my life?" Have a breakdown of what you will be doing more and what will be done less. Tell your inner self the truth that needs to be told. This is you looking forward to the future of positivity. This is a sure way to get started.

1. Focus on one habit at a time

Since your habits didn't start all at once, you need to know that changing it won't be all at once either, as much as you want it to be. Try tackling one habit at a time. If your focus is to stop the negative attitude towards project execution, face it. Don't combine many things. It's even an unhealthy attitude to try doing many things together

Start with the habit you are most uncomfortable with. Don't be in a rush. Progress is what you are after. Once you know the course you are following, getting there won't be a problem.

2. Ask questions

Don't act as if you are a professional here. There are so many things that will be going through your mind. Ask! You might be wondering how you would survive the night without excessive alcohol. Ask: "What if I would survive the first four hours?" Asking questions should not be limited to you. The help of a therapist or psychologist could be of help. You could also find it helpful when you ask questions from someone who has stuck to the new habit you are about to learn.

Your curiosity might also want to know when you will be able to adapt to the new habit. Ask! This way, you can make up your mind since you know the "when," "how," and "why."

3. Start with a deadline

We have established that there is no need to rush through sticking to positive habits. But you can start small and at your own pace. Give yourself a deadline to try out the first habit. Let's say for twenty days. So, for the next twenty days, you won't make that specific habit you have decided to start with. And of course, you'd replace it with the positive one. You can monitor your progress with your fingers. Your fingernails can represent the first ten days. Get a designed nail sticker and fix it to your fingernails daily after successfully sticking to the positive habit. After the sticker must have been attached for the first ten days, start removing them daily till the end of the next ten days. This action plan will give you a sense of control. You will have been able to both personalize this exercise and at the same time give it a deadline.

4. Celebrate your progress

You have started on a "big cheque" "less work" model. The big cheque represents your aspired habit, while less work is your effort to make things better. Realize that your goal is big but achievable. Achieving your aim progressively shows that you have moved from the realm of fantasy to reality. So why not celebrate every purpose you achieve? Boost your motivation by celebrating every progress. This tells you that you can do more and even better.

5. Stay with the tune

The rhythm of the new habit has been on the air for some time. Make sure you continue to dance to the song. No other song should persuade you. You have to be consistent. You might not want to change your routine. Try to build your purposed habit according to your method. All you require to do is to put on the new initiative. You might be thinking of decluttering your wardrobe. You could effectively do this the very moment you want to dress up. Just pick your preferred dress and use the other hand to arrange the other suits. Remember, start small so that you won't be overwhelmed.

6.   Don't give too many options
Being specific on strategies to stick to your new habit is necessary. Once you decide on how you want to go about it, stick to the plan. The moment you start weighing many options, doubt may set in. You might even get confused and discouraged. You have decided to reduce your alcohol intake by taking one full lemon after a glass of beer. Good! Stick to it. There are many other important decisions to make than to begin to conflict the ones you have already made.

Chapter Seven: Taming The Mind

The human mind is naturally wild and always in need of an adventure. Because of this, it is necessary that you learn how to tame the mind and have it work to your advantage. This will help it work to your advantage and provide you with lots of positivity. One of the wisest teachers and psychologists of all time, Buddha, described the human mind as a monkey that is always jumping about screeching and chattering endlessly. We all have minds that never want to rest, always in need of something else. Just as a monkey is always in need of attention, the human mind to always want you to put your entire focus on it. It achieves its goals in different ways, such as overhanging, negative considerations, anxiety, and fear.

Due to the presence of this monkey mind, it has now become harder for us to live in the present. Most of our time as humans is spent either regretting about the past or living in fear of the future. Soon you discover that you have become unhappy, sad, naturally angry, and restless. It is time to calm down and tame the monkey in mind. After all, it is your mind, and you should make use of it like you actually possess it. Some simple benefits of taming your mind include:

- Clarity of mind
- Full happiness
- Better sleep
- Focus and concentration
- etc.

All of these are very excellent benefits, and you should not hesitate to embrace them into your life. But there are some minor steps I will show you to help you fully actualize this dream.

12 Essential Tips To Stop Overthinking And Control Your Mind

It might sound strange to you, but the truth is that you are probably addicted to thinking. You may have never started to consider it, but most of us do spend a lot of time thinking and overworking our minds. We think about what to eat for dinner, which seasons to continue on Netflix, why the world climate is changing so severely. We think about virtually everything. While thinking is an excellent and necessary venture, it can sometimes clog up the mind when it becomes too much. Most of the time, we never know that it has become too much, and that is where the problem lies. Thinking so much in your mind can become a slight disorder and turn you towards overwhelming anxiety. Your mind stays stressed, and peace begins to elude you. Practice these and come up with your testimony:

1. **Study your mind and find those things that cause you stress and anxiety**

There are different reasons for different people as to why they overthink. For some, it could be financial instability; for others, security reasons; and for still others, it could be a terminal sickness. You will need to find yours. Ask yourself the necessary questions why you overthink, and the times you are most likely to overthink. Take note of the major things you think of and the pattern in which all of those thoughts form themselves. If this is done diligently, your notes will help you figure out some of the major reasons why you are currently overthinking.

2. **Consider the things that make you overthink**

The question here is, how important are those things that make you overthink? What use will they play in your life is you continue to trouble your mind about them? Will it matter in four years or four months even? If the answer is no, you should snap out of it. Your mind is simply playing sad tricks with you, and you have to be the boss here. If they are not important, then you should stop thinking about them and focus your time on more important things.

3. **Make quick decisions**

Learn to make a quick decision and get the process over with. If you are a kind of person that can take hours trying to figure out what to eat for lunch, then this is for you. There should be a timeframe for decision-making in your life. If you are going for a vacation, do your research and settle the destination in one week. Don't allow it linger on and on and become a problem to you.

4. **Start the day on a proper note**

I have mentioned it before: bad mornings will most likely lead to a bad day. Take hold of your day from the morning and begin to eliminate any stressful thoughts that make want to raise their heads. You can do this by reading something that will uplift your spirit every morning, or you can practice meditation to calm your mind.

5. **Understand that overthinking is bad for your mental health**

Overthinking steals away all of your time and energy that should have been used for something more important. It leaves you drained and unable to achieve tangible results. By doing some of these things to your mental health, you become susceptible to anxiety and depression, which are some major triggers of suicides and suicidal thoughts.

6. **Don't get too excited**

Of course, people also overthink positive thoughts. For instance, you have just carried out a short survey of your business profit projection and have seen that you could get thousands of dollars richer before the year ends. You begin to imagine all the things you could do with the money, the good life you can finally have, and the things you can finally get rid of. These thoughts will consume you with baseless excitement to the extent that you might forget ideas and continue to ruminate on them over and over, basking in the beauty you imagine for yourself.

7. **Document your thoughts**

Get those thoughts out of your head and into a paper. It helps out sometimes. You can get a notepad close to your bed and jot down those thoughts that come to you whenever you are about to go into sleep. Once it has been put down, the brain will be forced to let go of it and free you.

8. **Adopt a more carefree lifestyle**

Sometimes it is best not to care. Sure, there are a lot of things that should bother you, but ask yourself how many times thinking over a situation has helped that situation. The chances are one in a million. So sometimes it is best you forget everything and live like a king. Distract yourself from your thoughts and try to practice happiness more often.

9. **Get busy**

The mind rarely ever has time to think when you are busy. Although it can still happen, that will only come as a form of distraction which I have taught you how to overcome. One major cause of overthinking is an unproductive mind. People who keep themselves busy hardly ever have enough time to allow them to mind wander towards baseless thoughts.

10. **Realize that you can't control everything**

There are things that you can control, and there are others that are simply out of your control league. You have a journey tomorrow, and the weather forecasts that it will be a rainy day. There is no need to stress yourself over it. Cancel the trip if need be and have peace of mind.

11. Purge Your Environment of overthinkers

Your environment may play a significant role in triggering overthinking. It doesn't just stop at the people close to you. It extends to the things you read, the podcasts you listen to, the trends you follow, etc. Remove all of these from your immediate environment.

12. Live in the present (not in the past or future)

The only things that should bother you are those things that are presently going on in your life. If you are in college, focus on your studies and get good grades. Prepare for the future and stop bothering about it. If you were molested as a child, find a way to forgive and move on with your life. It can be hard, but remember, it is all for you.

7 Techniques To Conquer The Fear Of Failure

It is natural to fear failure. Failure is never something that one would want to be associated with, and so humans shake in their boots at the sight of it. Once we are pushed outside of our comfort zone, we begin to feel that things can probably go wrong. And the truth is that failure's sting is painful and it can leave you with a blemish for the rest of your life, except if you are a person that heals quickly and moves on fast. Understand that your failures are always a springboard to your success. You might be running out of time, but that is enough reason why you should do away with the fear of failure and instead calm down. Without darkness, you will never understand light. Without cold, you will never appreciate the heat. Without failure, you will never understand the true essence of success. So, there is no need to fear failure per se. But conquering the fear of failure isn't as easy as that.

You need to understand and put some things in place to fully gain the upper hand. Some of these include:

1. **Understand that failing doesn't mean that you are a failure**

A lot of people have failed a lot of times, but today we don't see them as failures. The examples are numerous.

- Nobody knows how many times Edison tried until he was finally able to invent the incandescent light bulb. But it is believed that it was more than a hundred times.
- An editor once told Walt Disney that his animations lacked imagination. Today, the Walt Disney company has more than fifty hugely successful animated films under its belt.
- J.K. Rowling's Harry Potter series was rejected more than ten times by different publishers until luck found her. Today she is the wealthiest author alive.

There are more examples, but the bottom line is that failure is never an endpoint except if you have decided for it to become your endpoint.

2. **Learn from your failures**

No matter how negative and experience is, there is always something positive to learn from it. It is only a fool that makes the same mistake twice. Sieve out all of our failures and select the benefits. They are there. You only have to look deeper and catch them. One way that can help you out is to begin to write out all the ventures that you failed in and write out the things you may have learned from failing in them.

3. **View any sight of failure as a challenge to step up your game**

If you think you might fail, take up the challenge, and prepare yourself not to fail. That is the only way to success. In fact, only a handful of people are totally sure of success when they first started out a venture.

Most of the time, they were quite pessimistic, but they put in their best and hoped for success. Success hardly eludes people like that, except if there was a mistake made somewhere.

4. Stay optimistic and keep visualizing success

Push the thought of failure away from your mind by stay positive and thinking positivity. The thought of failing will surely come, but what if you succeed? There are two sides to this coin, and none of them should be neglected while viewing the coin. If one out of every hundred business startups in our community survives more than five years, then it could be your startup. If only one person succeeds, then it could be you.

5. Understand that the fear of failure doesn't make you a success

No matter how much you sit about achieve nothing because of failure, success will never pity you and come to your rescue. Oh, you think the fear of failure is a heavy burden to bear? Try the burden of regret and see how far that will carry you. There is nothing as painful as seeing somebody achieving the things you had always wanted to achieve, just because you allowed the fear of failure to hold you back. Shove failure off you back and make a move.

6. Be kind to yourself

If you have ever experienced failure people before, it is time to get over it. Learn from your failures and get over it. Your mind might want to keep reminding you about how bad you are, telling you that you will never be good at anything. Instead, be kind to yourself. If you made a mistake in the past, promise yourself not to go down the same part again. Then forge ahead. Nobody is ever above mistakes.

7. Avoid perfectionism

Nothing in the world is ever perfect. Every beautiful thing in the world is laced with some flaw or the other. Recognize that nothing you will ever do will be downright perfect, so go ahead and start up something. Complete the task with the mistakes and then take the time to correct the mistakes. Completing the project itself is one great step, and this will give you the urge to carry on.

6 Secrets For Creating A Success Mindset

There can never be success without a success mindset. Those two go together like smoke and fire. There can never be one without the other. Think about most of the successful people that you know. The chance that they enter into success by mistake is pretty slim. A lot of the time, people who have a failure mindset always end up in failure, because they hardly ever identify opportunities whenever they meet them. A failure mindset will always work against you. No matter how much you try, no matter all the hard work you put in place, a mind running on failure will always produce failure. One major factor that differentiates great achievers from failures is the way they think, the content of their minds. So, to create the success you need, you need to prepare your mind for it. A failure mindset will always be shocked when success is finally achieved, but a success mindset will see success coming from a mile off. These secrets will help you develop the perfect mindset that will accommodate success:

1. Achieve small goals one at a time

When you look at your one big dream, the size of it might scare you into thinking you might fail in the long run. Remember that the large success picture does not appear at the snap of a finger. Rome was not built in a day. It was built one stone at a time. What are the stones that will build your future? Start putting them in, one block at a time. You want to win the Nobel Prize in Physics, then, you have to have a college degree in Physics first. You want to become a Pulitzer Award

Stop Procrastination

winner for Fiction; then, you must begin writing that novel now. These small blocks will build into one great mountain of success.

2. **Take charge of your mind**

We have touched little about this in Chapter 7 (taming the mind). It is easier for the mind to envision failure than to envision success. Close your eyes and imagine a plain ground, a desert without any form of life. See how easy that is to do? Now close your eyes and imagine that desert with skyscrapers, with people of all races engaging themselves in commerce. Imagine that this desert contains the tallest building in the world. See how hard it is for your mind to create a picture of wealth and abundance. If you succeeded, it must have taken you a conscious effort to do so. This is the kind of effort required to see your life as a success.

3. **Be flexible and ready to tweak your plans**

There is no hundred percent success plan in the world. Things can go wrong and show you the flaws in your plans. At this point, the best thing to do is to keep your mind ready for a change. It is possible that you will not achieve all the goals you attached to a plan, and that is ok. All you have to do is make sure that your mind is always ready for a change of plan.

4. **You are your biggest competition**

Always strive to get ahead of yourself. Know your destination and find out how fast you should move, then, move in that pace. Measuring yourself to the achievements of others can leave you with detrimental consequences. You can look up to people who have gone ahead of you and admire their lifestyle. Learn from them and keep trying to develop yourself.

5. **Find a Mentor (someone that will keep you motivated)**

A mentor is someone who acts like a parent to you or a master in any given field or endeavors you may find yourself. Put yourself in positions where you get to meet the best of the best in your field. Then build strong relationships with them that will turn into a mentorship. A mentor will be someone you can easily report yourself to if you make a mistake. A mentor will both scold and advise you whenever needed. And knowing that you have someone you can always look up to will provide with the needed dose of success mindset to keep you going.

6. **Talk to yourself**

The best advice you can get is the one you give to yourself. Sit yourself down and talk to you. Ask all the necessary questions and try to find out why things are working out the way that they are supposed to. The key here is that you have to be truthful with yourself. Take time and encourage yourself. Reward yourself. Appreciate yourself. Tell yourself you have to work harder and achieve better results. These will continually drive to achieve more at any given time.

Chapter 8: Planing For Your Success

The general public does not have the same definition of success, but in a broad view, doing well in the course of action can be tagged as a success. Some are of the school of thought that success has the right outcome from a decision; a superb result after an intention is fulfilled. However you define as successful living, be sure that some elements must be seen in it. Some of them are dedication, goal setting, motivation, and problem-solving. None of these traits will be found on a path to fulfillment if you don't understand the intent behind success.

Understanding your intent gives a sense of direction. You now have a decision tool to work with. You could predict where you are coming to your destination. You may ask, "What pushes me to set those unattainable targets? Why do I envision to become muscular? "Maybe I just stumbled on it," you may reply. Ask yourself many of these questions. Comprehend what moves you. From here, the energy to keep moving towards the rough road of attainment is fueled continuously. You may not need another person to push you to fulfillment. You and the inner drive will be enough motivation to get going.

Well, success is intentional, and you could get prepared for it. That's what this chapter promises to unleash.

6 Techniques To Succeed At Goal Setting

1. See the birds before the sky

Don't get me wrong here. We live in a world of no limitations, and everything is possible. But you need to see the things that are closer to you first before you can reach out to things beyond. Go for a goal you can easily attain. No rule says you must start in a hard way. And you don't have to be so complicated when planning for your goals. Achieve the little ones you can now, and the motivation will keep you inspired for the bigger ones.

2. **Expand your horizon**

Get your imagination to work. See yourself beyond the present level you are now. Until your inner self is motivated to achieve greatness, it will be difficult, if not impossible, to go far. Access as much information as possible to hit your goals. A better way to map out your plan is when vitality is added to the specific target.

3. **Admit your setbacks**

Aiming for perfection comes with loads of experience. You would not be experienced all at once in a day. What you call constant failure is what sets you on the peak. For you to move forward in fulfilling your goals, accept at every point when you fail. Acknowledging failures allows you to review your actions as well as find solutions for them. Unless you take your wrongs, you can't see the right.

4. **See it the other way round**

There is no cause to beat around the bush when the solution seems far. Don't get too complacent about your goal attainment. If you are stuck at an end, think of other ways to go about it. Be flexible! Sometimes, your deadline might have exceeded beyond a reasonable doubt. Get yourself going. Remember that what you want to achieve is still possible. If your goal is to study five chapters of a book in five days, and at the end of the sixth day, you are still in chapter four. Do not be discouraged and don't feel wrong about not meeting your target. Pick up the section for the next day. Ensure you review the cause of the delay and move on.

5. **Be result-oriented**

What should drive you is the success behind the goal. You will likely face distractions. It may come from your workplace, environment, or friends. Whatever it is, it shouldn't you stop from what you have set your mind to achieve. Think and position your brain for positivity. See every challenge as an avenue to become better. Visualize your results even before attaining them. Create a sound memory for yourself. Take pictures of what you tag as a success. Hang it around you, and let it encourage you now and then. It will not only boost your alertness; it will also make the journey to attainment fun

6. Don't get distracted

When it comes to priority, goals are not seeds of different fruits in a basket. They should be seen as fruits of a seed. Give preferences to what you want to achieve, and allow it to give birth to other goals. This approach ensures that you are orderly in your way to secure productivity. One big distraction you won't see coming is when you are trying to do many things at a time.

5 Less-Known Goal-Setting Tips Straight From The Experts

To fetch a glass of water seems more relaxed than setting a goal sometimes. But it may seem so difficult after writing your targets, and not attaining them. It might be a long-term goal or short-term. Yours might range from career to life goals. All the same, frustration may set in when none of these look attainable. The following tips will guide you to succeed in goal setting.

1.   Understand yourself
Socrates emphasized the subject of "self-knowledge." He believed that no one could be helped without self-identification. Although, major upgrades in science and technology has given a lot of answers to these worrying questions. Nonetheless, the wisdom behind getting to know the kind of human being you are is essential. It is a factor to consider

for one to be successful in the course of attaining targets. Do a quick analysis of your components.

- Start by asking questions

What are you made of? Why do I think differently from others? What causes me to get anxious over little subjects? Why do I get nervous anytime I see strangers? Questions like this could not be asked until you have taken time to think of some things you often do. The aim here is not for you to feel inadequate or depressed. It is just for you to get better.

- Analyze your findings

Check your social, spiritual, health, physical, psychological, and intellectual capabilities. A game of comparison will not work here. This check is for you! What am I capable of doing? And at what pace am I capable of doing it? What makes me learn fast with little energy? "I think I sleep faster whenever I take cereals." "Oh! I doze off almost immediately whenever I rub lotion on my feet." Analyzing will give you enough reasons why you do what you do.

- Make more findings

Don't stop at your discovery. Do more research online. Find out if the traits you saw in yourself is found in other people too. How were they able to overcome it? Was it by themselves, or were they helped by a friend or professional? Is this a childhood behavior or it accompanies growing up to adulthood? Getting answers to those questions, and many more you would like to add gives you a sense of identification.

- Combine factors

You could make a temporary conclusion base on your findings. By now, you are sure that what you feel and how you feel is reasonable. Maybe what you discovered has shown to you that you need help. Good! You are making progress. Don't combine any information if you have not researched extensively. Put each of these inputs together and help yourself with it.

2. Have a clear definition of your goal

What we sometimes see as a path can sometimes be blockage. We may tend to see possibilities at achieving a goal, but in the end, the result appears disappointing. Here is the reason. Humans have failed to properly decide without any form of prejudice what they want out of life. It is not as easy as we think, but this is what makes the goal attainment frustrating.

- Identify the difference

Just because it is achievable does not mean it has the same strategy as other goals. Understand the difference between what is to be achieved in a short while and what is to be met for a lifetime. Define what your goal is in your terms. What someone considers as a short-term goal may be a long-term goal for you. A long-term goal cannot be achieved if it is not broken down into smaller bits. There is no technicality in this at all. A short-term goal is what you want to reach over a short period while a long-term goal will take a more extended period to attain (it can be for months or years). Your friend, who dreams of becoming a chartered accountant, may plan to go to business school for that purpose. If you are not aware that going to business school is a strategy to pursue a career goal (which is to become a chartered accountant), you might follow suit and get frustrated at the end.

- Strategize and break down the difference

For every future, there is always a day to start it. That day is the present day you are in right now. And in a full day comprises of hours, minutes and seconds. Do a justification of what is to be done presently (at this very second) that will help the next 1,220 hours that you have set the deadline.

Stop Procrastination

What you should have accomplished in the next few days should not be muddled up with next years'. You don't have to get worried over the next decade when you can successfully fulfill the project for the next day.

Your action plan might be to extract a picture of a baby and gum it at the back of your door together with an adult image. Seeing those pictures should remind you of this guide.

- Have a clear direction

This point is where decision-making is essential. Gain the confidence to know what you want. Don't forget that your composition is not only psychological. You have to be specific enough in each area of your life.

- Decide and define what you want

What do I want in life? What do I want out of life? Ask yourself those questions. Money or comfort? Some might say both. But the truth is that what we want is a comfort. And we feel that getting the kind of pleasure we want needs money to achieve it. That's true! The idea is this: We don't want our bodies to be stressed. We want our vacation to be around the cutest places around the world. The sea view apartment has always been our dream residence. Those kinds of comforts that riches can get might not sit well with some people.

Giving to orphanages gives some people relief. Donating to NGOs might give confidence to some. So, define what you want and don't get confused because of someone else's needs. Your discovery should not be stacked to your head alone. Help yourself by writing it down. Your journal or diary might be a great friend to gist with.

- Identify the process involved

Attaining a goal is not automatic. It doesn't come as we project many times. There are steps to take to be successful in it. Ensure that you maximize each process fully before going to the next. You might have set a target to read three chapters of book per day. Until you have mastered consistency in reading those three chapters, you shouldn't think of increasing your reading goals to five chapters.

- Fill the gap

Get motivated to keep going. Whenever it seems like you have missed your routine to attaining goals, get a substitute to make up for it. It might involve doing a review or progress check on your previous goals. You might decide to get more information about what you have been doing recently. Ensure that you are not lagging. Note that you are not supposed to take this as a perfect excuse for shirking responsibilities.

3. Take the first step and continue

Nothing can be as hard as having the courage to begin. Having made a proper analysis of who you are, and what you are capable of doing, you are well aware of your mental and intellectual capabilities now. It is time to put them to work.

Start with your skills. Everyone has something they are good with. And you are no exception. Commit your passion to your skills by discovering what will help you to do more. Our aim here is for you to channel those skills to ease your goal setting

4. Get a model

Imagine how a child thinks when he is writing with a pencil. It's easy at first, because his hand was held while writing. Attaining goals can be the same when there is a structure to follow.

- External model

Life is practical, so is everything that exists in it. Your big motivation might spark up from getting a life model. This model is someone who has excelled in your proposed project. You might decide to choose a leader from your workplace or in your social group. The attributes of a leader should be more inspirational than a boss. Discover one in the path of your pursuit. It might even be at your religious gathering. One of the beautiful things to discover in a model is the ready-made pattern to follow. It is more like having a template to work with. With it, life becomes more real to you. You will tend to find proper guidance on what you do.

- Be your greatest asset

It is good that there is someone around to check on us. But the biggest motivation we would get is the energy from within us. No one can encourage you more than yourself. Inspire yourself to greatness. See yourself as a helper and the one that needs help. It is a contemporary approach to solving the problem. You are both the counselor and the client. Think of the kind of advice you would give to a distressed friend. Give such to yourself when you are in distress. It might not come easy at first. Don't forget that this is your first attempt. A better way to make it go well is for you to write down crucial advice you have given before. You should be able to devise relevant admonitions that have lifted people's spirit at one time. Use them for yourself. Also, think of the congratulatory message you sent to your relative at a time when he/she did something spectacular. Say it to yourself too.

5. Review your progress

Always have it in mind that your development is significant. Do a routine review of your goal. Ask relevant questions such as the process, the resources, sacrifice, and time involved. Don't pretend as if you have not been doing anything. Go through the first tip in this section again, and apply it to your review strategy.

7 Important Steps To Plan For Success

Successful living is not accidental. And to break the barrier of failed principles, you need a new awareness. Define your success, understand the purpose, and we can both work on a plan. This approach will help open up the ability to affect change in your life. It has to come as a choice for personal development.

1. **Get ready mentally**

There are realities to successful living, and one of them has to start within us. You need to be prepared mentally. This means that you have settled your mind on achieving success. And being successful is the only option you have. Prepare your mind to execute a different task that will require sacrifice. There will be a reshuffle of time spent, friends to hang out with, and certain things to do at a particular period. Create that positive mindset to overcome any challenges when it surfaces. You might need to develop many skills that you are not familiar with. Be ready to embrace failure as a stepping stone to become better. Quitting should not be an escape route to failure.

2. **Maintain an expressed goal**

Being specific about the kind of success you want is a better way to plan it. Express it by writing it down. You might decide to make it more professional. Structure it as a statement. Let it be as transparent as possible. Combine the right words that will set your foot running. Don't write any statement that seems too general. Let it unveil your intention to achieve results.

3. **Employ resources**

It is expected that confusion will set in during the journey of success. Getting ready for such is a way to show that we are prepared for it. Seek out for influencers around you. Some people have been where you are planning to be. Discover one of them and subscribe to their teaching. Go online and sign up for emails that are relevant to your plans. Listen and follow TV shows that deal with finance and investment. Streaming several videos on YouTube wouldn't be a bad idea either.

4. Secure a plan

By now, you should have been able to gather enough knowledge to give you an edge. Design a strategy that will most fit you. Don't forget that you don't need to generalize your methods, and starting small is something you shouldn't forget so soon. Realize the opportunities that lie in fulfilling every strategy and take it.

5. Invest in time

By now, you should have been able to identify your priorities. Priority is very crucial in planning for success. You don't just focus on a thing without creating extra time to make it work. During this time, do more research about your plans, review them, and meditate over them. Learn what you need to know about specific action and develop yourself in it.

6. Boosters

See and create enough motivation to keep you going. Start with your willpower. Settle every inner craving. You don't want to have setbacks again, do you? No! Then, set boosters for yourself. Don't forget that no one can give you true happiness than yourself. The same thing is real with motivation. Have reasons to find joy in your strategies to success, and that's why it is best to adopt a plan that most fits you. You may extend a bit of your motivation to your friend. This action will work well when you report your progress to them, and at every development, they reward you (based on mutual consent).

You might go the extra mile of creating what I tagged as "progress competition." It means trying to get better results at every little success. This effort will always bring consciousness to become better because you continuously see the next achievement as an upgrade to the previous. Your focus here is to ensure the consistent improvement in every course of action

7. Learn from tactics

The world revolves around ideas, and through that, innovations are born. Study world leaders and successful individuals. There are specific attributes that make them stand out in their respective fields. You may adopt some of their principles. If it performed for them, it would surely be a perfect guide for you too.

30 Day Step-By-Step Plan To Help You Build Habits And Fire Up Your Productivity

I believe that you have had a most amazing time going through the contents of this book. Some of the things that have listed here are small bits of the things you can do to fire up your creativity. By now you should be putting things in place to be able to conquer your distractions, create more focus and stay motivated. We know that random practices do not easily lead to success. There has to be a set-down plan to get the best out of ever set of instructions. Because of this, I have decided to gift you this 30-day step-by-step plan to enhance your creativity, motivation and productivity. This plan is loaded with small points that will change your life one day at a time for the next thirty days. All you have to do is follow it strictly and don't falter at any point, no matter how weary you may get.

This aspect of the book has been broken down into 30 parts, representing the thirty days in which the steps will be taken. You might wonder if it is really necessary to take it one day at a time. Well, it is up to you. If you have already conquered one day of the plan, you can move over to the next. Even after experiencing success, please do not forsake the instructions contained here. Go over them from time to time, probably every 60 days or as you may see fit. Take this as a guide. You know yourself best and you know how these guidelines will suit. Do not hesitate to modify them however you see fit. Don't forget to stick to every habit you are developing during these thirty days. It will change your life. I wish you success.

Day 1	Day 2

Morning
  1. Exercise the body for about 10 minutes.
	Morning
	  1. Clear work desk at work.
	  2. Skip and exercise the body for twenty minutes.

2. Listen to a motivating podcast. 3. Eat a well-balanced diet from the list of highly energetic foods (example: Brown rice and Sweet Potatoes). 4. Get the mind to work. Afternoon 1. Study the task at hand and try to identify the benefits open to me if I am able to complete the specific task. 2. Have a short power nap. 3. Read a book and refresh the mind.	3. Repeat some positive affirmations to myself. Afternoon 1. Try to find ways and reasons to love my job even better. 2. Break major tasks into bits. 3. Set a timeframe to complete each bit of broken-down tasks. 4. Do away with anything that may present itself as some sort of escape route from the task at hand.
Day 3	Day 4
Morning 1. Clear work desk at work. 2. Skip and exercise the body for twenty minutes. 3. Repeat some positive affirmations to myself. Afternoon 1. Study the task at hand and try to identify the benefits open to me if I am able to complete the specific task.	Morning 1. Listen to a motivating podcast. 2. Clear work desk at work. Afternoon 1. Let off a little steam doing something fun like listening to music, taking a walk with the dog, or conversing with a co-worker. 2. Have a short power nap if I feel tired or a little

2. Have a short power nap. 3. Read a book and refresh the mind. Evening 1. Make a short assessment of my major life goals and see how far I have come towards achieving them. 2. Evaluate the day and scold myself of any mistakes made.	stressed out. This will help replenish my mind. 3. Try to reduce the workload at hand by pushing some to a later time. Note: You are not procrastinating. You are only trying to provide your mind with the necessary clarity needed to complete a particular task. Evening 1. Reread chapter six of this book and find out how well I have been coping with the instructions.
Day 5	Day 6
Morning 1. Creatively combine any of the energy boosting foods listed in chapter one. Afternoon 1. Break major tasks into bits. 2. Set a timeframe to complete each bit of broken-down tasks. 3. Do away with anything that may present itself as some sort of escape route from the task at hand. Evening	Morning 1. Listen to a motivating podcast. 2. No screen time until I complete a major task. Afternoon 4. Study the task at hand and try to identify the benefits open to me if I am able to complete the specific task. 5. Have a short power nap. 6. Read a book and refresh the mind. Evening 1. Evaluate the day and scold myself of any mistakes made.

1. Evaluate the day and scold myself of any mistakes made. 2. Make important decisions for the next day this evening.	2. Go through chapter four of this book and remind yourself of its contents.
Day 7	**Day 8**
Morning 　1. Creatively combine any of the energy boosting foods listed in chapter one. Afternoon 　1. Take a short power nap. 　2. Eat brain fruits like blueberries. 　3. Spend one hour completing a major task. Evening 　1. Spend the evening brainstorming with people in my field who can be good mentors. 　2. Figure out practical ways in which I can connect to them and make them pick interest in helping me out.	Morning 　1. Meditate for 10 straight minutes. 　2. Clean and declutter my home and workspaces to give myself some form of clarity. 　3. Perform the most tedious task this morning. Evening 　1. Create a list of activities for the next day. 　2. Read one chapter from any book. 　3. Watch an inspiring video.
Day 9	**Day 10**
Morning	Morning

1. Listen to a motivating podcast. 2. Creatively combine any of the energy boosting foods listed in chapter one. Afternoon 1. Break major tasks into bits. 2. Set a timeframe to complete each bit of broken-down tasks. 3. Do away with anything that may present itself as some sort of escape route from the task at hand. Evening 1. Go through chapter one of this book and remind myself of its contents.	1. Take a glass of water first thing this morning. 2. No screen time this morning until I have completed one particular task completely. Afternoon 1. Call my mentor and talk to them about my progress. 2. Complete one part of a major task. Evening 1. Read chapter two of this book and assess how well I have followed the instructions. 2. Answer emails and reply messages.
Day 11	Day 12
Morning 1. Meditate for 15 straight minutes. Afternoon 1. Take a short power nap. 2. Eat brain fruits like blueberries.	Morning 1. No screen time until 9am. 2. Begin a major task. Afternoon 1. Take a short power nap. 2. Eat brain fruits like blueberries. 3. Spend one hour completing a major task.

3. Spend one hour completing a major task. Evening 1. List out things I am grateful for. 2. Reward myself with something pleasurable.	Evening 1. Go through chapter seven of this book and remind yourself of its contents. 2. Go to bed early for the next morning.
Day 13	Day 14
Morning 1. Creatively combine any of the energy boosting foods listed in chapter one. 2. Call my mentor and find out how they are doing. Afternoon 1. Go for a 10-minute break and refresh the mind either with a chapter from a book or a short inspirational clip. Evening 1. Make a to-do list for the next day. 2. Make a list of things to be thankful for. 3. Take stock of any progress made during the day.	Morning 1. Show gratitude for the good things in my life. 2. Make a short assessment of my major life goals and see how far I have come towards achieving them. 3. Produce a clearly defined strategy for the day ahead. Afternoon 1. Stay conscious and try to identify the major causes of my laziness. 2. Go through chapter eight of this book and remind yourself of its contents. Evening 1. Make a to-do list for the next day. 2. Make a list of things to be thankful for. 3. Take stock of any progress made during the day.
Day 15	Day 16

Morning 　1. Listen to a motivating podcast. 　2. Halfway through the 30-day plan: Assess myself and find out how well I have fared. Afternoon 　1. Start an important task and timeframe for this task to be completed. 　2. Take a short power nap. Evening 　1. Go out and spend the night with a friend or colleague.	Morning 　1. Get the mind to work by engaging in some mind games. 　2. Clear work desk at work. 　3. Break down all large projects into smaller ones. Afternoon 　1. Take a short power nap. 　2. Eat brain fruits like blueberries. 　3. Spend one hour completing a major task. Evening 　1. Evaluate and find out how much I have covered towards achieving my goals.
Day 17	Day 18
Morning 　1. Creatively combine any of the energy boosting foods listed in chapter one. 　2. No screen time until 9 AM. Use the time to finish up a major task. Afternoon 　1. Go through chapter seven of this book and remind yourself of its contents. 　2. Take a short power nap. 　3. Eat brain fruits like blueberries.	Morning 　1. Creatively combine any of the energy boosting foods listed in chapter one. 　2. Complete the hardest tasks of the day this morning. Afternoon 　1. Try to find ways and reasons to love my job even better. 　2. Break major tasks into bits. 　3. Set a timeframe to complete each bit of broken-down tasks. 　4. Do away with anything that may present itself as

Evening 1. Go out and have fun. 2. Appreciate myself for any success recorded.	some sort of escape route from the task at hand. Evening 1. Make a short assessment of my major life goals and see how far I have come towards achieving them.
Day 19	Day 20
Morning 1. Go through chapter two of this book and remind yourself of its contents. 2. Creatively combine any of the energy boosting foods listed in chapter one. Afternoon 1. Break major tasks into bits. 2. Set a timeframe to complete each bit of broken-down tasks. 3. Do away with anything that may present itself as some sort of escape route from the task at hand. Evening 1. Talk to myself and address any form of fear of failure lingering in my mind. 2. Reaffirm some of the quotes listed in	Morning 1. Listen to a motivating podcast. 2. Creatively combine any of the energy boosting foods listed in chapter one. Afternoon 1. Browse the internet and the study the lives of one successful person I admire. Evening 1. Make a list of major changes in my life since the beginning of the 30-day plan. 2. Reward myself.

	chapter three of this book.
Day 21	**Day 22**
Morning 1. Creatively combine any of the energy boosting foods listed in chapter one. 2. Start up a major task. Afternoon 1. No screen time until 3 PM. 2. Continue with the major task from the morning. Evening 1. Go out and reward yourself.	Morning 1. Listen to a motivating podcast. 2. Meditate Afternoon 1. Take a short power nap. 2. Eat brain fruits like blueberries. 3. Spend one hour completing a major task. Evening 1. Make a short assessment of my major life goals and see how far I have come towards achieving them.
Day 23	**Day 24**
Morning 1. Get the mind to work by engaging in some mind games. Afternoon 1. Try to find ways and reasons to love my job even better. 2. Break major tasks into bits. 3. Set a timeframe to complete each bit of broken-down tasks.	Morning 1. Listen to a motivating podcast. 2. Exercise for 10 minutes. Afternoon 1. Take a short power nap. 2. Eat brain fruits like blueberries. 3. Spend one hour completing a major task. Evening

Stop Procrastination

4. Do away with anything that may present itself as some sort of escape route from the task at hand.	1. Go out for a night with a colleague or friend.
Day 25	**Day 26**
Morning 1. No screen time till 9 AM. 2. Start on a major task. Afternoon 1. Study the task at hand and try to identify the benefits open to me if I am able to complete the specific task. 2. Have a short power nap. 3. Read a book and refresh the mind. Evening 1. Go through chapter six of this book and remind yourself of its contents. 2. Complete a major task.	Morning 1. Creatively combine any of the energy boosting foods listed in chapter one. Afternoon 1. Study the task at hand and try to identify the benefits open to me if I am able to complete the specific task. 2. Have a short power nap. 3. Read a book and refresh the mind. Evening 1. Make a short assessment of my major life goals and see how far I have come towards achieving them.
Day 27	**Day 28**
Morning 1. Creatively combine any of the energy boosting foods listed in chapter one. 2. Assess my long-term plan and find out	Morning 1. Meditate for 10 minutes. 4. Go through chapter eight of this book and remind yourself of its contents. Afternoon

217

Day 29	Day 30
those that are not producing results. 3. Brainstorm new ideas and plan to create a better solution. Afternoon 1. No screen time until I complete a major task. 2. Task a short power nap. 3. Go for a walk and refresh my mind. 4. Carry out exercise four and the focus exercises listed in chapter five. Evening 1. Reward yourself for the day. 2. Assess yourself and find out how successful you have been throughout the week.	1. Study the task at hand and try to identify the benefits open to me if I am able to complete the specific task. 2. Have a short power nap. 3. Read a book and refresh the mind. Evening 1. Make a short assessment of my major life goals and see how far I have come towards achieving them.

Morning 1. Creatively combine any of the energy boosting foods listed in chapter one. Afternoon 1. Go through chapter three of this book and remind yourself of its contents. 2. Complete a major task before having any screen time. Evening 1. Call my mentor and ask for advice on some specific points of concern. 2. Make plans on how to implement the advice given.	Morning 1. Get the mind to work by engaging in some mind games. 2. Creatively combine any of the energy boosting foods listed in chapter one. Afternoon 1. Study the task at hand and try to identify the benefits open to me if I am able to complete the specific task. 2. Have a short power nap. 3. Read a book and refresh the mind. Evening 1. Make a short assessment of my major life goals and see how far I have come with achieving them. 2. Make assessments and see how far you have come in the 30-day plan.

Conclusion

It has indeed been a journey, and I believe that you have been motivated to get over procrastination and fire up your productivity. But remember, doesn't end there. You have to put in your efforts to achieve success finally. It is one thing to read an excellent book and be motivated, and it is another thing to put into practice everything that has been taught. It is action that differentiates a winner from a loser. So, which will it be for yours? Will you finish this book and forget everything that was taught? I hope not, because that would be a disaster. Begin to apply all of the tactics and techniques that have been listed and see your life change for the better.

I have simplified the instructions contained in this book for you, in the form of a 30-day plan. Follow the instructions given day after day, and follow it consistently and religiously. Remember that change is a gradual process. You might not notice the change on the first day, but with time you will see that you are no longer the same person. Research has proven that any action carried out consistently for more than 21 days finally becomes a habit. So, to create the habit of productivity, you have to follow the laid-out steps I have provided you. At the end of the 30 days, you will notice a great change in your life and have a testimony share with your friends.

I wish you success and more productivity in your life as you take action today. Remember, your mind is under your control.

www.ingramcontent.com/pod-product-compliance
Lightning Source LLC
Chambersburg PA
CBHW031107080526
44587CB00011B/859